Pasta
all the recipes

G GIUNTI DEMETRA

Project design and layout: Laura Casagrande

Translation: Helen Cleary and Helen Glave for Lexis, Florence

Editing: Catherine Frost

Illustrations: Archivio Giunti/© Claudio Innocenti, Florence

Credits:

All the pictures belong to Archivio Giunti/© Giuliano Valsecchi but the following:

Archivio Giunti/© L. Borri pp. 51, 139d; Archivio Giunti/© R. Germogli pp. 21, 63, 77, 149;

Archivio Giunti/© Stockbyte (CD-RF) pp. 83, 87;

© Cazals Jean/The Food Passionates/Corbis p. 109;

Fotolia: © Lorenzo Buttitta p. 67, © Marco Meyer pp. 69, 89, © Francesco83 p. 73, © Giuseppe Porzani p. 95, © JJAVA p. 121, © Silvana Comugnero p. 131, © Riccardo Spinella p. 132c, © Promolink p. 132s, © Lapas77 p. 132d;

© Photocuisine/Tips Images pp. 93, 117;

© Stockfood/Olycom pp. 19c, 27, 81, 105, 125, 155;

© Nico Tondini/Marka p. 111.

The publisher declares himself willing to pay any amounts due for photographs
for which it has been impossible to determinate the source.

www.giunti.it

© 1999, 2012 Giunti Editore S.p.A.
Via Bolognese 165 - 50139 Florence - Italy
Piazza Virgilio 4 - 20123 Milan - Italy
New edition: March 2012

Reprint	Year
7 6 5 4 3	2018 2017 2016 2015

Printed by Giunti Industrie Grafiche S.p.A.
Prato (Italy)

Contents

3

Pasta, vegetables and cheese

Baked pasta

Gnocchi and filled pasta

5

Home-made pasta

Sauces and dressings

Introduction

ALL IN ONE DISH

◆

Since pasta is the true cornerstone of Italian cooking, we have decided to devote an entire cookbook to some of the best-known Italian pasta dishes.

We have selected some of the most famous regional dishes as well as tasty, original ideas and suggestions that transcend regional boundaries.

If our baked lasagna is not exactly the one your Italian grandmother made, it might be the one your best friend's grandmother made. Each recipe, in fact, has many variations according to region, province, or the inspiration of the cook. That's what makes Italian cooking so surprisingly good and the same dish, though extraordinarily savoury, is never identical; but be sure that wherever you are in Italy you will enjoy any pasta dish you eat.

We hope these recipes will also stimulate your creativity so that, rather than following the instructions to the letter, you can produce your own version of a dish, using secret ingredients that make it truly special.

ITALY = PASTA

◆

The invention of pasta, a dough made of cereal mixed with water, goes back a long way. Traces of this food have been found in Etruscan bas-reliefs, and in Greek and Roman texts. What is certain is that dry pasta was eaten during the Arab domination of Southern Italy, long before Marco Polo came back from the Orient (1292) with his tales of Chinese soya spaghetti.

Originally, pasta came in simple shapes (*vermicelli* or *maccheroni*, *spaghetti*, *tagliatelle*) and it was only later that more imaginative formats evolved. At the same time, pasta began to be filled and transformed into *tortellini*, *ravioli*, and *agnolotti*. The dough could also be modified to produce several types of *gnocchi*.

The first sauces were made of spices, honey, milk or vegetables. Only with the great sixteenth-century voyages of exploration did tomatoes arrive in Europe, along with aubergines, peppers, and many other vegetables. At first, the tomato was thought to be a fruit having magical properties. It was the Sicilians who turned it into a sauce, creating the classic dish 'pasta with tomato sauce'.

This brings us to the nineteenth century. Nino Romano writes: 'In 1800 the first pasta factories were founded. In 1811 tomato concentrate, better known as "black conserve" was produced in Parma. [...] In 1835 the first important factory for the production of bottled tomato sauce was opened in Boston. In 1900, with the introduction of electrical energy, the production process was developed still further.' (*Le ore della pasta*, Ed. Acanthus).

Pasta has become a symbol of Italy the world over, and the red-white-and-green dish of spaghetti is recognised everywhere as a message of joy and good cooking.

MEDITERRANEAN DIET, BALANCED DIET

◆

In the 1950s, with the economic boom and a new wave of affluence, Italians abandoned their traditional eating habits.

In keeping with the image of 'humanity immersed in the frenetic rhythm of modern life' created by progress, Italians turned increasingly toward the American eating style, shunning traditional dishes with their embarrassing memories of peasant life.

Out went pasta, bread, and rice; in came meat, pre-cooked, ready-to-eat foods and colourful, super-filled sandwiches. Italians too learned to eat on the run. Rapidly losing the habit of the leisurely midday meal, more and more people preferred fast-food snacks in a café. Wine and water went out of fashion, replaced by sodas and soft drinks.

With progress came the so-called afflictions of affluence – heart disease, cholesterol, hypertension, arteriosclerosis and obesity. Science laid the blame on stress, unnatural life rhythms, and sudden changes in lifestyle. The branch of science that studies nutrition has confirmed the existence of a definite link between eating habits and health.

To keep in good health, you need to choose an eating style that is well-balanced and complete. The diet that best meets these requisites is the traditional, Mediterranean, Italian peasant diet, which Italians had begun to reject as out-of-date and old-fashioned.

Eating quickly and on the run is bad for the health. Instead, you should take time to sit down at a table to foods such as cereals, vegetables, fruit, fish, dairy products, vegetable oils and a little meat.

The Mediterranean diet not only contributes to physical and mental health, but is also advantageous from an economic point of view, since no costly ingredients are needed.

PASTA
WITHOUT GAINING WEIGHT

◆

The principle of the Mediterranean diet does not consist exclusively of eating Italian products, but also knowing how to select, to provide balance, and combining foods correctly for proper nutrition. In the last ten years, fashions in beauty have turned increasingly towards an ideal of thin, long-limbed, evanescent men and women. For someone with the Mediterranean physique, this look can be attained only by following strict diets that banish pasta from the table. Apart from the futility of pursuing a physical ideal imposed by advertising, eliminating some foods from the daily diet is a threat to the health of our organism, which needs numerous precious elements. Among these, carbohydrates, abundantly present in cereals (60%), provide a major source of energy.

Whether you have a weight problem, or just want to keep fit, it is useless to follow a restrictive diet. Often, in fact, the kilos lost through hard sacrifice reappear the minute you go back to a normal diet. This not only exerts a negative effect on the body, but also influences the nervous system.

Robert Salvatori writes: 'The solution to being overweight is in our own hands; you only need to tackle the problem with common sense and determination.' (*La Dieta Mediterranea*, Idea Libri). It is not by changing traditional eating habits that we keep fit, but by following moderation and balance in our daily diet.

In regards to the dishes in this cookbook, there are around 360 calories in 100 g of pasta – very little, when you consider that our daily requirement is 2,500-3,000 calories. You just need to keep an eye on portion size, the sauce that goes with the pasta, and the other foods that follow in the meal.

BALANCE AND MODERATION

◆

Ideally, you should give your body all the elements it needs in the right quantities, by distributing carbohydrates, proteins, vitamins, mineral salts, fats, etc. over three daily meals (breakfast, lunch, dinner).

A plate of cereals included in your menu will supply your body with carbohydrates, minerals and enzymes (particularly if you use organic whole-grain pasta), which can be supplemented by a plate of vegetables, best flavoured with extra-virgin olive oil. The small amount of protein in pasta (11%) can be compensated with the addition of legumes, a little meat, fish or cheese. A first course of pasta, with a sauce made of vegetables and other ingredients containing protein, is a full meal in one dish that will satisfy your appetite as well as your bodily requisites.

Traditional Italian dishes, especially those based on pasta, fully comply with the principles behind the re-assessment of the Mediterranean diet. It should be remembered, however, that Italian traditional cooking comes mainly from the peasant world, where dishes were hardy and filling to provide energy for long hours of physical exertion.

In the affluent society, much less energy is expended in a day. We travel very little by bike, and even less on foot. Work often involves sitting for hours behind a desk or in a car. Consequently, we should reduce the amounts of some of the ingredients used in preparing pasta dishes.

Progress has not been wholly negative, however. While introducing new products, it has focussed new attention on those we had forgotten. We can now prepare a traditional lunch while skilfully avoiding, through substitution, any less digestible or less suitable ingredients, without giving up what food represents: health and pleasure.

If you sometimes get carried away, it's a good idea to follow (or precede) a sumptuous meal with a light snack to aid the work of the stomach by allowing it to digest the superfluous food. As for exercise, try to include a few stairs in your daily routine, or an hour's walk, or biking to work and back. The rewards of eating right are a sense of well-being, a relaxed, fit body and an uncluttered mind.

THE RIGHT SAUCE

◆

As mentioned, a plate of pasta does not make up a large part of our daily calorie allowance (100 g dry pasta = 200-250 g cooked pasta = 360 calories). But this does not permit us to eat as much as we want. Smaller helpings of pasta, from 60 to 80 grams, can be followed by moderate portions of other foods, giving our body everything it needs without overdoing it.

Sauces and added ingredients should be chosen carefully, since they are strictly linked to the caloric value of a plate of pasta.

Substituting a sauce or reducing its amount is mainly a question of taste. The recipes found on the following pages appear in their traditional versions. For instance, you will find lard as well as butter.

Whenever possible, use **extra-virgin olive oil** as a substitute, and always cold-pressed. Extra-virgin olive oil, produced by mechanical olive pressing and without chemical manipulation contains less than 1% of its weight in acidity (expressed as oleic acid). It is produced merely by washing, sedimentation and filtration. This type of oil provides a dressing that is rich in unsaturated fatty acids. Due to its chemical composition, it undergoes only minor alterations in cooking, which are harmless.

Sauces and dressings based on animal fats should instead be used frugally and carefully. Butter, for example, apart from being rich in saturated fats, becomes toxic at high temperatures (200 °C).

FOOD COMBINATIONS

◆

To keep any food from becoming toxic, hard to digest and harmful to the metabolism, it should be combined correctly with the other components of a meal. The stomach does not secrete only one type of gastric juice, but juices that are 'personalised' depending on the kind of food to be digested. When we eat starch (rice, pasta, bread etc.), the stomach produces a slightly acidic (neutral) gastric juice. Whereas, when instead we eat protein (meat, cheese, etc.) the digestive process requires a very strong enzyme activated by hydrochloric acid.

If not limited by special occasions (the pleasure of transgression cannot be denied), bad food combinations can result in the fermentation and putrefaction of food in the intestine. This can cause a number of digestive problems (heartburn, colitis, etc.) as well as a weakening of the immune system. Other than the classical association of pasta plus meat (which is a kind of a single dish that should be followed by a light second course or just salad), among the ingredients that can be used with pasta we find:

• **Legumes:** the protein they contain supplements that of the pasta, which is poorer in quality and lacks some essential amino acids.
• **Vegetables:** raw or cooked, they can be combined with pasta in large quantities. The only precautions should be taken with potatoes (also rich in starch), spinach and tomatoes (acidifying foods).
• **Fruit:** depends on the acidity and maturity of the fruit. In any case, this combination requires caution and should only be used occasionally. The same applies to oily fruit.
• **Cheese:** avoid low-fat cheeses, preferring ripe, slightly fatty cheeses.
• **Milk:** not easy to digest with pasta but can be used occasionally.

This does not mean, of course, that you should totally avoid tasty dishes that might conflict with the principles of combining foods. You just have to go easy, not overburdening the stomach with starters or sweets, keeping servings small, and helping the digestion along by taking a little exercise after the meal.

PASTA:
TYPES AND FORMATS
◆

Pasta is simply the result of mixing water with flour (obtained by milling wheat). There are two types of wheat:

durum wheat, which when milled produces *semola* and *semolato*, and common wheat, which when milled gives white flour. Dry factory-made pasta produced industrially is generally made of durum wheat flour, and this guarantees its durability, firmness when cooked, and taste. Since durum wheat is more expensive, it is usually mixed with **common wheat**. Italian law specifies that the dry pasta sold in shops cannot have more than 7% common wheat flour, while foreign brands entirely ignore this restriction. It is easy, however, to identify the brands to be avoided.

Good quality dry pasta is recognisable by its yellowish colour, its slightly sweet flavour and the fact that it is odourless. It can be stored for a long time in a dry, dark place. Fresh pasta can be kept for a shorter time (a few days only) and should be refrigerated. The packets should be kept closed to protect against dust and insects.

Whole-grain pasta deserves special mention. This factory-made pasta is left untreated by refining processes. Refinement deprives the flour of those natural properties of the wheat that make it a balanced element: protein, sugar, fats and mineral salts, vitamins and enzymes. Be careful, however, to choose only whole-grain pasta produced from wheat grown without the use of anti-mildew or other toxic products, which leave a residue on the grains of wheat.

Further care should be taken to choose pasta that is really made of whole-grain flour and not merely common flour to which bran has been added. The latter will not have a uniform amber colour but rather a freckled appearance that reveals the presence of added bran.

Both regular and whole-grain pasta are found in the shops. Their different characteristics appear on the labels.

• **Regular, dry pasta:** produced with durum wheat flour
• **Dry egg pasta:** this includes 200 g of eggs for each kilo of flour.
• **Coloured fresh or dry pasta:** made of flour coloured with a percentage of spinach, dried or powdered tomatoes, tomato concentrate or eggs (200 g per kilogram of flour).

• **Special dry pasta:** produced with flour to which has been added a percentage of malt or gluten to increase the protein value to 15-20%.
• **Fresh pasta:** can be made of durum wheat flour alone, common wheat flour alone, a combination of both, and/or other ingredients.

There is also a range of diet pastas in the shops, for babies, diabetics, etc. Always look for the trustworthy brands (which are not always the best known) when it is not possible to buy from hand-made pasta shops. Sometimes, to economize, chemical additives and colorants or other ingredients are used in place of eggs.
In Italy, it seems, there are 500 different pasta formats, and still today imaginative producers are creating more new types to tantalise the eyes and taste buds of the consumer. In general, the formats available can be grouped as follows:

• **Long, rounded pasta** with varying diameters: (*vermicelli, spaghettini*), and sometimes hollow (*bucatini, zite*);
• **Long narrow ribbon-like pasta** such as *trenette, linguine, bavette*;
• **Long, wide pasta:** *lasagne, pappardelle, reginette*;
• **'Nests' or 'coils' of pasta:** *capelli d'angelo, fettuccine, tagliolini, tagliatelle*;
• **Medium-short pasta:** *penne, conchiglie, ruote*;
• **Short, thick pasta:** *maccheroni, sedanini, fusilli*.

RULES FOR A GOOD PLATE OF PASTA

◆

• Choose the pasta format in relation to the sauce you plan to make: the bigger the pasta, the richer the sauce. *Capelli d'angelo* can be flavoured with oil (or butter) and cheese, whereas *zite* are better served with meat sauce, cream, mushrooms, etc. and short thick pasta is ideal for oven-baked dishes.

• The pasta should be cooked in plenty of water (around 1 litre for each 100 g). If you are cooking less than half a kilo of pasta, the pasta/water ratio changes; for example for 4 people calculate 350 g pasta and 4 litres of water. Bring the water to the boil in a large, deep pot so that the heat is evenly distributed. The liquid should never reach the brim of the pot because pasta can swell to three times its dry volume while cooking.

• Add salt only when the water has begun to boil, calculating about 10 g salt for every litre of water. Salted water, in fact, boils at a lower temperature than fresh water.

• Add the pasta to the pot, a little at a time, when the water is already boiling. As soon as the water comes to a boil again, lower the heat to a simmer. An exception to this rule is filled pasta, which is added to the pot a minute before boiling so that it will not be broken by the motion of the water.

• Stir the pasta regularly so that it cooks evenly and does not stick. A useful hint, especially for egg or filled pasta, is to pour a little oil in the water before adding the pasta.

• Drain the pasta when it is al dente; the less water it absorbs, the tastier and more digestible it will be. If the pasta is to be tossed in the pan or baked au gratin in the oven, drain it slightly before it is fully cooked.
For the cooking time, apart from the indications given on the packet, you can trust in the old 'taste test' (if there is a little white dot in the middle of the spaghetti, it needs to be cooked 1 minute longer).

• Having turned off the heat, stop the cooking process by pouring a glass of cold water into the pot, then drain the pasta in a colander. If you are cooking gnocchi or another delicate pasta, drain with the aid of a slotted spoon or a large fork, transfer to a deep dish, tip up and let the excess water drain out with the help of a lid.

If the pasta is to be tossed in the sauce, or if stipulated in the recipe, leave it in a little of its cooking water so that it will mix better with the sauce.

• For stirring the pasta, cooking the sauce and mixing the ingredients together, always use wooden utensils to avoid the risk of toxic substances or unpleasant flavours contaminating the food, and to avoid breaking the pasta.

• Traditionally, pasta is dressed in the following sequence: drain the pasta, transfer it to a serving bowl with some grated cheese in it (optional), then fold in the sauce, mixing gently and carefully to blend the ingredients.

CARE
WITH OTHER INGREDIENTS

◆

Some final words of advice before you begin to cook. All the ingredients, not just the main ones, should be **fresh** and of the **best quality**. If you have the chance, use products (including meat, eggs, butter, etc.) that are grown or raised by natural methods, without the use of chemical substances or procedures. Make sure that fish, in particular, is fresh, and caught in clean water.

Nature offers the cook an inexhaustible source of flavours in the form of **aromatic herbs**. Garlic, basil, bay leaves, fennel, mint, marjoram, hot red peppers, etc., are small but very important ingredients that express personality on your dish of pasta. Get to know them well to use them in the best ways possible in your recipes. Do not mix too many aromatic herbs together in the same dish, and always use them in moderation, so as not to overwhelm the flavour of the other ingredients.

Remember too that the salt most commonly used is produced by dubious refinement processes and is composed almost exclusively of sodium chloride. Refinement processes deprive it of the vital elements it originally contained,

which, even in a small percentage, can have important biological effects. The salt used in the following recipes is not refined salt but **sea-salt**, now readily available in both the coarse and the fine form. This salt, not subjected to refinement processes, is rich in elements such as chlorine, sodium, magnesium, sulphur, calcium, potassium, bromine, carbon, strontium, silicon, fluoride, zinc, phosphorous, etc.

18

CONVERSION CHART

WEIGHT AND LENGHT	CORRESPONDES TO	
1 gram (g)	0.035 ounces (oz)	divide by 28 to find ounces
1 hectogram (hg)	3.57 ounces (oz)	divide by 0.28 to find ounces
1 kilogram (kg)	2.2 pounds (lb)	divide by 0.45 to find pounds
1 millilitre (ml)	0.03 fluid ounces (fl oz)	divide by 30 to find fluid ounces
1 litre (l)	2.1 pints (pt)	multiple by 2.1 to find pints
	3.8 gallons (U.S.) (gal)	divide by 0.26 to find U.S. gallons
	0.22 gallons (U.K.)(gal)	divide by 4.5 to find U.K. gallons
1 centimeter (cm)	0.4 inches (in)	multiple by 0.4 to find inches
1 millimeter (mm)	0.04 inches(in)	multiple by 0.04 to find inches
1 meter (m)	3.3 feet (ft)	multiple by 3.3 to find feet
TEMPERATURE		
Celsius degree (°C)	180 °C = 356 °F	(°C x 1.8) + 32 to find Farenheit degree
Farenheit degree (°F)	392 °F = 200 °C	(°C -32) x 555 to find Celsius degree

NOTE
The quantities in the recipes on the following pages are for 4-6 servings.

Pasta

with meat

20

BIGOLI WITH DUCK

◆

400 g bigoli (recipe on page 137), 1 small duck, 1 carrot, 1 onion, 1 celery stick, 2 cloves garlic, 1 bunch aromatic herbs (bay leaf, rosemary, parsley, basil), 300 g tomato purée, about twenty black olives (optional), halved and pitted, 1/4 litre of dry white wine, extra-virgin olive oil, salt and pepper.

Clean the duck and sear it, then lightly brown it together with a mixture of chopped carrot, celery, garlic, the herbs and several tablespoons of olive oil. Add the wine and let it evaporate, then add the tomato purée and season with salt and pepper. Simmer for about 2 hours in a covered pot over moderate heat. If necessary, add a little hot stock or water from time to time.

When the duck is cooked, take it out of the pot, remove the bones, slice the meat and set aside. Pass the cooking juices through a food mill and add the halved olives. Continue cooking the sauce for around 15 minutes, then put the meat back in the pan and heat well. Use the sauce to flavour the bigoli, which have been cooked in boiling salted water and drained when al dente.

BUCATINI ALL'AMATRICIANA
📷

400 g bucatini, 200 g pancetta, 300 g ripe and firm tomatoes, 1/2 onion, stock, extra-virgin olive oil, grated pecorino, salt, ground hot red pepper.

Blanch the tomatoes in hot water, peel them, remove the seeds and chop. Chop the bacon and brown it in several table-

spoons of oil. As soon as the fat has rendered, remove the bacon from the pan and set aside. Chop and sauté the onion in the same oil. Add the tomatoes and salt, and let the sauce thicken for about ten minutes. Put the cooked bacon back in the sauce and flavour with ground hot red pepper. Use the sauce to flavour the bucatini, cooked in boiling salted water and drained when al dente. Sprinkle generously with grated pecorino. Since the original recipe had little or no tomato, this ingredient can be omitted if preferred.

BUCATINI WITH LAMB AND PEPPERS

◆

400 g bucatini, 200 g lamb, 500 g tomato pulp, 2 red or yellow peppers, 2 cloves garlic, 1 bay leaf, 1/2 glass dry white wine, extra-virgin olive oil, salt, ground hot red pepper.

In an earthenware pot, protected by a heat diffusing plate, flavour several tablespoons of oil with crushed garlic and a bay leaf, then add the diced lamb and let it brown. Remove the garlic cloves and add the wine, letting it evaporate over high heat. Clean the peppers, remove seeds and inner filaments, finely chop, and add to the lamb. Cook for a few minutes, then add the tomato pulp. Bring the sauce to the boil over high heat, then lower the heat, cover and simmer until the meat is done. Before removing from the heat, check the seasoning and flavour with ground hot red pepper. Cook the bucatini in abundant

salted water, drain when al dente, and drizzle with oil. Transfer to a serving dish and dress with the sauce.

BUCATINI MARCHIGIANI
◆

400 g bucatini, 100 g mixed Parma ham and bacon, 400 g tomato pulp, 1 onion, 1 carrot, 1 celery stick, red wine, grated pecorino, extra-virgin olive oil, salt and pepper.

Chop together the onion, carrot and celery and sauté in a pan with a little oil. Add the sliced Parma ham and bacon, moisten with wine and let evaporate. Add the tomato, a little salt and pepper and cook for around 30 minutes. In the meantime, cook the bucatini, drain when al dente, transfer to a warmed soup tureen or serving dish and flavour with the sauce. Add a generous sprinkling of grated pecorino and serve piping hot.

CAVATIEDDI WITH HAM
◆

400 g cavatieddi (recipe on page 133), 500 g ripe and firm tomatoes, 100 g Parma ham in one slice, 1 onion, 1 carrot, 1/2 stick celery, red wine, extra-virgin olive oil, grated pecorino, salt, ground hot red pepper.

Dice the ham. Chop together the onion, carrot and celery and sauté in oil in an earthenware pot. Add the diced ham, stir and cook for a few minutes, then add the wine. Continue cooking until the wine evaporates. Peel the tomatoes after blanching them in hot water, dis-

card the seeds, chop and add to the mixture. Add salt and a pinch of ground hot red pepper; simmer for around 20 minutes. Cook the cavatieddi in abundant salted water, drain when al dente and flavour with the sauce and a generous sprinkling of grated pecorino.

FARFALLE WITH TURKEY AND PEA SAUCE
◆

400 g farfalle (butterfly-shaped pasta), 200 g turkey breast, 100 g bacon, 500 g ripe and firm tomatoes, 200 g fresh hulled peas, 1 onion, marjoram, extra-virgin olive oil, salt and pepper.

Chop the onion and sauté it with the chopped bacon in several teaspoons of oil. Cut the turkey into thin slices and add it, stirring gently to let the flavours blend. Soften the peas in boiling salted water, then add them in. Blanch the tomatoes in boiling water, peel them, remove the seeds, chop and cook together with the peas. Let the sauce thicken; season it with salt, pepper and marjoram. Continue cooking, adding a few drops of water from time to time if the sauce becomes too dry. Cook the farfalle in boiling salted water, drain when al dente and mix with the sauce.

FETTUCCINE ALLA PAPALINA
◆

400 g fettuccine (recipe on page 138), 100 g thinly sliced Parma ham, 200 g small peas, 2 eggs, 1/2 onion, 2 1/2 tablespoons grated Parmesan, extra-virgin olive oil, salt, freshly ground pepper.

Sauté the chopped onion in a few tablespoons of oil over high heat, add the peas and season with salt and pepper. Lower the heat, cover and let simmer, adding a little hot water from time to time if necessary. Just before removing the pan from the heat, cut the ham into smaller slices and add to the peas. In the meantime, beat the eggs together with the Parmesan, a pinch of salt and some freshly ground pepper in a warmed serving bowl. Cook the pasta, drain when al dente, pour into the warmed bowl and add the pea sauce. Mix well before serving.

FETTUCCINE ALLA ROMANA
◆

400 g fettuccine (recipe on page 138), 300 g beef, 500 g ripe and firm tomatoes, 1 onion, 1 carrot, 1 celery stick, 1/2 glass red wine, 2 teaspoons lard, salt, ground hot red pepper.

Dice the beef. Sauté the chopped onion, carrots and celery in the melted lard, add the diced beef and sprinkle with hot red pepper.
Add the wine and let it evaporate. Peel the tomatoes, remove the seeds, chop and add to the beef sauce. Add salt to taste and continue cooking. Boil the fettuccine in salted water, drain when al dente, transfer to a serving bowl and serve piping hot, dressed with the meat sauce.

FILATIEDDI WITH LAMB SAUCE
◆

400 g filatieddi (recipe on page 137), 800 g lamb shoulder, 500 g ripe and firm tomatoes, 80 g dried mushrooms, 1/2 onion, 2 teaspoons chopped parsley, 1 pinch ground hot red pepper, 60 g grated pecorino, 2 teaspoons flour, 1/2 glass dry white wine, 10 g lard, 1 1/2 tablespoons extra-virgin olive oil, salt.

Dice the lamb. Melt the lard in a saucepan, add the diced lamb, season with salt and ground hot red pepper, cover and simmer over low heat for 25 minutes. In the meantime, soften the dried mushrooms in lukewarm water for about 15 minutes, drain and slice. Remove the pieces of lamb from the pot, keeping them warm. Add the oil and mushrooms to the cooking juices in the pot. Cook over moderate heat for a few minutes. In a separate bowl, pass the tomatoes through a food mill and set aside. Remove the mushrooms and mix with the lamb. Add the finely chopped onion to the cooking juices, stir and cook until transparent. Add the wine and let it evaporate. Remove from the heat, stir in the flour, then put back over the heat. As soon as the flour starts to brown, add the tomatoes, season to taste and simmer for 20 minutes. Put the lamb and mushrooms back in the pot, cover and cook for another 10 minutes. Lastly, add the chopped parsley. Cook the pasta in boiling salted water, drain when al dente, and blend well with the sauce. Sprinkle generously with grated pecorino.

FUSILLI WITH SAUSAGE AND PORCINI MUSHROOMS

◆

400 g fusilli (short, curly pasta), 200 g sausage, 300 g fresh porcini mushrooms or 30 g dried mushrooms, 300 g tomato pulp, 1 onion, 1 small carrot, 1 bay leaf, marjoram, extra-virgin olive oil, salt and pepper.

Clean the mushrooms carefully and dice. If you are using dried mushrooms, steep them first in lukewarm water. Chop the onion and carrot and sauté them in a few tablespoons of oil. When the onion is transparent, add the skinned and sliced sausage, the mushrooms and the crushed bay leaf.
Cook for a few minutes stirring gently, then add the tomato pulp, salt and pepper. Lower the heat, cover the pot and simmer until the sauce has thickened. If necessary, add some hot water or stock from time to time (or use the liquid in which the mushrooms have been steeping, strained through a cotton cloth). Before removing from the heat, flavour the sauce with finely chopped marjoram.
For a different flavour, combine the sausage with artichokes. Remove the spiny ends and tough outer leaves from the artichokes, cut into wedges and soak in water and lemon juice before adding to the mixture of onion and carrot in the pot. In either case, the sauce used to dress the fusilli should be very hot.

GARGANELLI ALLA BOSCAIOLA

◆

400 g garganelli (recipe on page 137), 200 g porcini mushrooms, 150 g thick-cut bacon, 4 ripe tomatoes, 1 clove garlic, 30 g butter, 1 sprig parsley, Parmesan cheese, salt and pepper.

Clean the mushrooms with a soft brush or a damp rag without rinsing in water. Sauté the sliced mushrooms, chopped bacon and crushed garlic in butter over medium heat, while stirring with a wooden spoon.
Blanch the tomatoes in hot water, peel them, remove the seeds, chop and add them to the mushrooms and bacon. Cook over low heat until the sauce has thickened and remove the garlic.
Boil the garganelli in abundant salted water, drain when al dente and transfer to a large serving dish. Add the sauce, garnish with chopped parsley and sprinkle generously with grated Parmesan. Serve immediately.

GARGANELLI SAPORITI

◆

400 g garganelli (recipe on page 137), 100 g ground beef, 1 cup tomato sauce, 1 cup béchamel sauce, 1 leek, 1 sprig rosemary, extra-virgin olive oil, Parmesan cheese, salt and pepper.

To the oil add the rosemary, sauté the finely chopped leek until transparent. Add the ground meat, a pinch each of salt and pepper, and let brown. Add the tomato sauce and cook until thickened. Boil the garganelli in salted water, drain and transfer to the pot with the sauce. Add the béchamel and mix well. Remove from the heat, sprinkle with Parmesan cheese and serve piping hot.

MACCHERONI WITH MEAT BALLS

◆

400 g maccheroni, 200 g ground beef, 500 g tomato pulp, 1/2 onion, 1 small carrot, 1/2 celery stick, 1 bunch parsley, 1 bay leaf, 1 clove garlic, basil, 1 1/2 tablespoons grated Parmesan cheese, breadcrumbs from 1 stale roll, 1 egg, milk, extra-virgin olive oil, salt, ground hot red pepper.

Soften the breadcrumbs in a little milk and squeeze out the moisture. Add them to the ground beef with a little parsley, crushed garlic, a sprinkle of grated cheese, a pinch of salt and one of hot red pepper. Mix all the ingredients together carefully, binding with the an egg yolk. If mixture is too soft, the meatballs will crumble in the sauce.
Form little balls about the size of a large olive and brown them evenly in the oil; when they have turned golden, drain and set aside.

Clean the pot and put it back over the heat with 1-2 table-spoons of new oil and a mixture of diced onion, celery and carrot.
Sauté the vegetables; when wilted, add the tomato pulp, salt and bay leaf and continue to cook. A few minutes before turning off the heat, remove the bay leaf, add the meatballs to the sauce along with a little hot red pepper and the chopped basil. Stir to blend the flavours, then remove from the heat.
Boil the maccheroni in salted water, drain when al dente, and mix with some of the sauce. Spoon the remaining sauce over the pasta and sprinkle with abundant grated Parmesan.

MACCHERONI WITH SAUSAGE AND RICOTTA

◆

400 g maccheroni, 400 g ricotta, 150 g sausage, grated pecorino, extra-virgin olive oil, salt and pepper.

Skin the sausage and brown it over low heat in its own fat. Cream the ricotta in a large bowl with salt, a generous grinding of pepper and the sausage. When the mixture is rich and creamy, set it aside and cook the pasta in abundant salted water.
Drain the maccheroni when al dente, reserving a few spoonfuls of the cooking water. Transfer the pasta to a serving

dish with the ricotta and sausage mixture and mix carefully with the salted water, a sprinkling of grated pecorino and a drizzle of oil.

MALLOREDDUS
WITH WILD BOAR SAUCE
◆

400 g malloreddus (recipe on page 134), 450 g ground wild boar, 450 g tomato sauce, 1 onion, a few bay leaves, grated pecorino, extra-virgin olive oil, salt and pepper.

Sauté the onion in a generous amount of oil, add the ground meat, flavour with a pinch each of salt and pepper, and brown for a few minutes. Add the tomato sauce with a few bay leaves and simmer for 2 hours. After cooking the malloreddus in abundant salted water, drain and flavour it with the sauce and the grated pecorino.

ORECCHIETTE
ALLA LUCANA
◆

400 g orecchiette (recipe on page 135), 300 g ground veal, 500 g ripe and firm tomatoes, 1 onion, a few basil leaves, extra-virgin olive oil, grated pecorino, salt, ground hot red pepper.

Finely chop the onion and sauté until transparent with a few spoonfuls of oil in an earthenware pot. Add the ground meat and salt, stir and cook for a few minutes.
Blanch the tomatoes in boiling water, remove the skin and seeds, then sim-

mer over low heat for about 2 hours, stirring from time to time. If necessary, add a little hot water. Before removing from the heat, check the seasoning, add a little hot red pepper and the crushed basil.
Boil the orecchiette in abundant salted water, drain and dress with the sauce and a sprinkling of grated pecorino.

PAPPARDELLE
WITH VENISON
AND PORCINI MUSHROOMS

400 g pappardelle (recipe on page 138), 350 g venison leg, 150 g porcini mushrooms, 1/2 litre red wine, 1 small onion, 1 small carrot, 2 bay leaves, 1 small sprig rosemary, 40 g butter, Parmesan cheese, salt and pepper.

Cut the meat into cubes and marinate in the red wine (keeping a glassful aside), the aromatic herbs and the roughly chopped carrot and onion for 12 hours.
When done, strain the meat, herbs and vegetables from the marinade. Mix the herbs and vegetables together and sauté in a little butter.
Clean the mushrooms with a soft brush or a cotton cloth. Finely slice them and sauté separately in a little butter. Stir in the meat cubes and brown over moderate heat for a few minutes. Add the glass of red wine, salt and pepper. Lower the heat, cover the pot and simmer for 30 minutes.
After 30 minutes, add the cooked vegetables to the meat and mushrooms.

Boil the pasta in salted water, drain when al dente and transfer to the pan containing the sauce. Sauté together for a couple of minutes and serve with a generous sprinkling of grated Parmesan.

PAPPARDELLE WITH WILD BOAR

400 g pappardelle (recipe on page 138), 400 g coarsely ground lean wild boar meat, 350 g tomato pulp, 2 teaspoons tomato concentrate, 1 small carrot, 1 onion, 1 celery stick, 2 bay leaves, 1 glass of red wine, extra-virgin olive oil, salt, ground hot red pepper.

In a little oil, sauté a mixture of finely chopped onion, carrot and celery, add the ground meat and let brown.
Add the red wine and let it evaporate. Mix in the tomato pulp and the tomato concentrate diluted in a little hot water. Add salt, ground hot red pepper and the bay leaves. Simmer over low heat for about an hour and a half.
Boil the pappardelle in salted water, drain when al dente and stir in the meat sauce before serving.

A variation to this recipe suggests using 2 parts boar meat and 1 part beef to lessen the gamy flavour typical of wild boar. You can also use only tomato concentrate, omitting the tomato pulp.

PAPPARDELLE WITH HARE SAUCE

◆

400 g pappardelle (recipe on page 138), 1 small hare, 50 g bacon, 1/2 onion, 1/2 celery stick, 1 small carrot, 1 clove garlic, rosemary, 2 teaspoons tomato concentrate (or 1.5 dl milk), 1 glass red wine, extra-virgin olive oil, salt and pepper.

Clean the hare, keeping the forepart (head and shoulders), heart and liver for the sauce.
Wash under cold running water, dry and cut into pieces, being careful not to break the bones.
In a few tablespoons of oil, sauté a mixture of chopped bacon, garlic, onion, carrots and celery. As soon as the vegetables begin to wilt, add the pieces of hare, including the entrails.
Allow meat to brown over moderate heat, add the wine and let it evaporate. Season with salt, pepper and rosemary. Continue cooking for a few minutes, then add the tomato concentrate diluted in a little hot water. Lower the heat, cover the pot and simmer for about half an hour. If necessary, add a little stock or hot water from time to time.
When the meat is done, take the pieces of hare out of the pot, remove the bones, and chop. Pass the sauce through a sieve, then put back over the heat, with the chopped meat and entrails.
Heat the sauce well before mixing in the pasta, which has been cooked in boiling salted water and drained when al dente. In another version of this recipe, milk can be used instead of tomato concentrate.

28

PAPPARDELLE WITH PHEASANT

◆

400 g pappardelle (recipe on page 138), 1/2 pheasant, 1 small glass of cognac, 1 glass dry white wine, 1 cup vegetable stock, a few sage leaves, 1 sprig rosemary, 60 g butter, 1 tablespoon cream, Parmesan cheese, salt.

Pluck and debone the pheasant. Clean and wash it under cold running water, dry the meat and slice it into small strips. Sauté in 30 g of butter with a few bay leaves.

When the meat is golden brown, add the cognac and white wine and let evaporate.

Lower the heat, cover the pot and simmer for half an hour, moistening with the hot vegetable stock from time to time.

Pass the pheasant liver and the cooking liquid through a sieve. In a separate pot, melt a little butter and flavour it with the rosemary.

Boil the pasta in abundant salted water, drain when al dente, transfer to the pot with the pheasant meat.

Add the liver and cooking juices, the melted rosemary butter and the cream and mix well. Sprinkle generously with grated Parmesan.

PENNE CUBAN STYLE

◆

400 g penne, 100 g cooked ham in one slice, 300 g fresh mushrooms, 300 g ripe and firm tomatoes (optional), 1 clove garlic, 1 small bunch parsley, 1/4 litre cream, extra-virgin olive oil, salt, ground hot red pepper.

Clean the mushrooms carefully with a brush or cloth and without rinsing, then slice them. Heat a few tablespoons of oil in a pan and flavour with crushed garlic. As soon as the garlic begins to brown, remove it and add the mushrooms to the oil.

If using tomatoes, blanch them first in hot water, peel them, remove the seeds and chop. Add the tomatoes to the pan, cover and simmer over moderate heat. If necessary, add a little salted water or hot stock.

In a separate bowl, mix the ham cut into cubes, the cream, a little hot red pepper and some finely chopped parsley.

Boil the pasta, drain when al dente and transfer to the pan with the mushroom sauce. Add the cream and ham and mix carefully. Serve piping hot.

PICI WITH RABBIT SAUCE

◆

400 g pici (recipe on page 135), 1/2 rabbit, 300 g tomato sauce, 100 g bacon, 2 celery sticks, 1 onion, 1 carrot, 2 cloves garlic, 2 bay leaves, 1/2 litre red wine, extra-virgin olive oil, salt and pepper.

In a large dish, marinate the rabbit overnight in the wine with the aromatic

herbs and the coarsely chopped vegetables. Next day, remove the vegetables, chop them finely and sauté in a little oil with some chopped bacon. Remove the rabbit from the marinade, cut it into pieces and add to the sautéed mixture.

Stir to let the rabbit meat absorb the flavours, then moisten with wine from the marinade and let it evaporate almost entirely.

Add the tomato sauce, season to taste, cover the pot and simmer over moderate heat for about an hour and a half. When the sauce is done, remove the rabbit, bone it and cut the meat into smaller pieces.

Blend the cooking juices to a creamy sauce, then put the pieces of meat back in it. Set aside to rest while you prepare the pasta. Boil the pici in salted water and drain when al dente. Put the sauce back over the heat, add the pasta and toss together for one minute.

PISAREI, PORK SAUSAGE AND PEPPERS

◆

400 g pisarei (recipe on page 136), 1/2 cotechino (pork sausage), 1 pepper, 1 clove garlic, 1 ladle tomato purée, extra-virgin olive oil, grated Parmesan cheese, salt.

Boil the pork sausage (if you are using a packaged traditional cotechino, follow the instructions on the packet; if you use home-made cotechino, keep it wrapped in a white cloth, sewn at the ends, while cooking).

Skin the sausage and dice it finely. Scorch the pepper on all sides in the oven, remove the burnt skin along with the seeds and inner filaments, then slice it.

Sauté the diced pork sausage in the oil with the pepper strips, garlic and a little salt. Add the tomato purée and cook for a few minutes.

Boil the pasta, drain when al dente, and transfer to the pot with the sauce. Sauté for a couple of minutes, sprinkle with grated Parmesan and serve hot.

PIZZOCCHERI WITH COOKED HAM

◆

400 g pizzoccheri (recipe on page 136), 150 g thickly sliced cooked ham, 40 g butter, 1 1/2 tablespoons single cream, 2 sage leaves, grated Parmesan cheese, nutmeg, salt.

Cut the ham into match-stick slices. Melt a little butter in a pan and add the sage leaves.

Cook the pizzoccheri in salted water, drain and transfer to the pan. Add the melted butter, the ham, the cream, the salt and some grated nutmeg. Mix all together and toss over moderate heat for two or three minutes. Serve immediately, sprinkled generously with grated Parmesan.

REGINETTE
WITH SPECK

◆

400 g reginette, 200 g thickly sliced speck (cured smoked ham), 100 g fresh hulled peas, 2 cloves garlic, 1/2 glass dry white wine, extra-virgin olive oil, grated Parmesan cheese, salt and pepper.

Blanch the peas in boiling salted water for about ten minutes, then drain. Cut the speck into cubes and sauté in a few tablespoons of oil with the sliced garlic cloves and the peas. As soon as the garlic begins to colour, remove it from the pan.
Add the wine to the peas and let it evaporate. Add salt and pepper and continue cooking over moderate heat for about ten minutes.
In the meantime, cook the reginette in abundant salted water, drain when al dente and transfer to the pot with the speck and peas.
Mix together over the heat for a few minutes, season with a grinding of pepper and sprinkle with grated cheese.
To vary this recipe, add 3-4 tablespoons of cream to the speck to bind the mixture together.

REGINETTE
WITH SNAIL SAUCE

◆

400 g reginette, 1 kg snails, 500 g ripe and firm tomatoes, 1 onion, 1 celery stick, 1 clove garlic, 1 bay leaf, 1 bunch aromatic herbs (rosemary, thyme, basil), 1 sprig parsley, 1 glass white wine, cornmeal, grated Parmesan cheese, extra-virgin olive oil, salt and pepper.

Clean the snails and prepare them for cooking. Boil them for ten minutes in salted water with some aromatic herbs. Plunge them into cold water to cool, then drain, remove the shells and clean away the entrails. Transfer the snails to a bowl containing the cornmeal and rub them with your hands in the bowl to get rid of any residual liquids. Wash again and dry. They are now ready for cooking.
In a pot (preferably earthenware), sauté the chopped onion, crushed garlic and bay leaf. Add the snails, stir well and add the finely chopped celery and parsley.
Cover the pot and let the flavours blend over low heat for several minutes. Moisten with the wine, raise the heat and let the wine evaporate. Add the tomatoes (previously peeled and chopped with seeds removed). Lower the heat and let the sauce thicken. Lastly, add salt, pepper and a handful of finely chopped aromatic herbs. Cook the reginette in salted water and drain when al dente. Serve in a warmed tureen, dressed with the snail sauce and sprinkled generously with grated Parmesan.

SPAGHETTI ALLA CHITARRA WITH RAGÙ SAUCE

◆

400 g spaghetti (recipe on page 136), 500 g pork in one slice, 4 slices of bacon, 1 piece of bacon fat, 500 g ripe and firm tomatoes, 3 garlic cloves, a small bunch parsley, red wine, 1 tablespoon lard, fresh pecorino, salt and pepper.

Chop two cloves of garlic with a little parsley, then mix with the chopped bacon fat and a little freshly ground pepper to form a paste. Spread the paste over the slice of pork, beaten thin with a meat pounder or the blade of a knife. Place the bacon slices over the paste and top with a few pieces of pecorino. Roll up the meat and fasten with toothpicks or kitchen thread.

Cut the remaining lard into pieces and melt in an earthenware pot along with the remaining garlic clove. Brown the meat, add a little wine and as soon as it has evaporated add salt and pepper. Peel the tomatoes, discard the seeds, chop and add to the meat.

Cook the sauce until done. A minute before turning off the heat, remove the meat and set it aside.

Boil the spaghetti in salted water, drain when al dente and flavour with the sauce. Slice the meat and serve it as a second course.

TAGLIATELLE WITH RABBIT SAUCE

◆

400 g tagliatelle (recipe on page 138), 200 g rabbit meat, 1 clove garlic, a few sprigs of rosemary, 2 teaspoons white flour, 1/2 glass dry white wine, extra-virgin olive oil, butter, salt and pepper.

Cut the rabbit meat into small pieces and marinate for an hour in wine, a little salt and pepper, and the shredded rosemary.

Remove the meat and brown it in a little oil that has been previously flavoured with the garlic clove. When the meat turns golden-brown, add the salt and cook until done, moistening now and then with some of the marinade.

Remove the rabbit meat from the pot and set aside. Add a tablespoon of butter to the cooking juices and stir in the flour.

As soon as the sauce thickens, put the pieces of rabbit back in the pot and stir in the pasta, which has been cooked al dente and drained.

TAGLIATELLE
WITH BOLOGNESE SAUCE

◆

400 g tagliatelle (recipe on page 138), 200 g ground beef, 50 g bacon, 1/2 onion, 1 small carrot, 1/2 celery stick, 1 1/2 tablespoons tomato concentrate, 1/2 glass red wine, grated Parmesan cheese, stock, extra-virgin olive oil, salt and pepper.

Finely slice the onion, carrot and celery. Slice the bacon and brown it in a few teaspoons of oil (not too much oil if the bacon is fatty). When the fat has rendered, add the chopped vegetables, stirring gently.

As soon as the vegetables have wilted, add the meat. Keep stirring until the meat is evenly browned. Add the wine and let it evaporate.

Add the tomato concentrate, diluted with a little hot stock and seasoned with salt and pepper. Lower the heat and simmer covered for about 2 hours. Moisten from time to time with a little hot stock.

Boil the tagliatelle, drain when al dente, and mix with some of the meat sauce. Serve with the remaining sauce in a sauce boat, and grated Parmesan on the side.

There are several variations to this dish. You can use mixed ground meats, or add some chopped chicken liver with dry mushrooms and the water used for steeping, or omit the tomato concentrate, and so on.

SPAGHETTI
ALLA CARBONARA

400 g spaghetti, 200 g bacon, 2 eggs and 2 egg yolks, 1 clove garlic, 2 tablespoons grated Parmesan cheese, 1 tablespoon grated pecorino, extra-virgin olive oil, salt and pepper.

Dice the bacon into 5 mm cubes and brown in a pan with a few tablespoons of oil and the clove of garlic (removing the garlic as soon as it begins to colour). In a warmed serving bowl, beat 2 whole eggs and 2 yolks at room temperature with the grated cheeses. Season with a pinch of salt and plenty of freshly ground pepper, and stir well to form a smooth, creamy sauce.

The sauce should be prepared when the pasta is almost done. Boil and drain the pasta, transfer it to the serving bowl, mix with the egg and the crunchy hot bacon and serve piping hot.

34

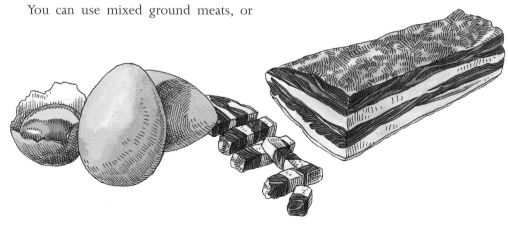

TAGLIOLINI
WITH CHICKEN LIVER SAUCE

◆

*400 g tagliolini (recipe on page 138), 300 g
chicken hearts and livers, 1/2 onion, 2 sage leaves,
2 teaspoons tomato concentrate or 2 tablespoons
cream, dry white wine, butter, salt.*

Finely chop the onion. Gently sauté it in
a pot with a spoonful of butter and the
sage leaves. Add the coarsely chopped
chicken hearts and let the mixture
brown. Remove the sage, add the wine,
and let it evaporate. If desired, add the
tomato concentrate, diluted in a little hot
water. Just before the hearts are cooked,
add the chicken livers, which have been
cleaned and coarsely chopped, add salt,
and let the flavours blend. If you prefer not to use tomato concentrate,
blend the cream into the sauce a minute before turning off the heat.
Cook the tagliolini in abundant salted
water and drain when al dente, then
fold carefully into the sauce and serve.

VERMICELLI
WITH CHICKEN
AND TRUFFLES

◆

*400 g vermicelli, 1 medium-sized white truffle,
1 chicken breast, tongue, 1 mozzarella, 150 g fresh
peas, 1 tomato, 1/2 glass meat roasting juices,
grated Parmesan cheese, butter or extra-virgin olive
oil, salt.*

This is a recipe with a variety of ingredients offering great scope to the im-
agination and taste of each individual
cook.
Cook the vermicelli in salted water and
drain them when they are al dente.
Dress with butter (or oil), grated Parmesan and the roasting juices.
Transfer to an ovenproof dish, shape the
pasta into a mound. Decorate it with
strips of chicken breast and tongue,
which have been cooked separately
with the fresh peas cooked in butter
and with slices of tomato, topping the
dish off with thin slices of truffle. Mix
in a little more of the roasting juices and
sprinkle with grated Parmesan. Cut the
mozzarella into slices and fan them out
over the pasta.
Place the dish in a hot oven until the
mozzarella begins to
melt. Serve hot from
the oven.

Pasta

with fish

BAVETTE
WITH FISH
◆

400 g bavette, 600 g mixed seafood such as baby squid, small cuttlefish, scampi and shrimp, 3 cloves garlic, a small bunch parsley, 1/2 glass of white wine, extra-virgin olive oil, salt, ground hot red pepper.

Remove any small bones or fins from the seafood as well as eyes, beaks or entrails (extracted by pulling the tentacles, taking care not to break the ink sac, which can be used to flavour this or another sauce).
Wash the seafood and if the bodies are large, cut them into small strips, leaving the little tentacles intact. Shellfish need not be shelled, just washed carefully. Cut the shrimp into pieces; the flesh can be eaten and the shell gives flavour.
In a large pot, heat a few tablespoons of oil with the crushed garlic and the hot red pepper; add the fish, heat it on all sides, then add the wine and let it evaporate.
In the traditional recipe, the bavette are broken, added

to the pan with the fish along with some boiling water, and cooked like risotto.
If this seems too complicated, boil the pasta as usual, drain when al dente and mix into the sauce before serving. In either cases, stir in a generous sprinkling of chopped parsley just before turning off the heat.

BIGOLI
WITH SARDINES
◆

400 g bigoli (recipe on page 137), 6 sardines, 1 clove garlic, a small bunch parsley, 1 glass of extra-virgin olive oil, salt.

In this typical dish from the Veneto Region, the sardines used in the traditional recipe were always fished in Lake Garda.
You can, however, use tinned sardines, which should be cleaned (without using water, if possible), deboned, and then treated like fresh ones.
Clean the sardines, removing the heads, bones and tails; wash them, let them dry on a teacloth, then cut them into small pieces.
Cook them in hot oil until they begin to disintegrate. Just before turning off the heat, add a mixture of chopped garlic and parsley.
Boil the bigoli in salted water, drain while still al dente and blend thoroughly into the sauce.

BUCATINI
WITH SQUID

◆

400 g bucatini, 4-5 squids (about 500 g), 500 g spinach, 500 g ripe and firm tomatoes, 200 g mushrooms, 1 clove garlic, 1 small bunch parsley, 1 egg, 1 1/2 tablespoons grated Parmesan cheese, 2-4 teaspoons breadcrumbs, extra-virgin olive oil, salt, pepper, ground hot red pepper.

Clean the vegetables, using a cotton cloth to remove the grit and soil from the mushrooms. Boil the spinach in salted water, drain and squeeze out the excess water.
Slice the mushrooms, sauté them in a few tablespoons of extra-virgin olive oil, season with salt and pepper. Mix with the cooked spinach.
Clean the squid; separate the tentacles from the body, discarding the entrails and taking care not to break the ink sacs. Chop the tentacles and mix with the vegetables along with a little chopped parsley, the egg, cheese, breadcrumbs, a pinch of salt and one of pepper. Mix well to form a smooth mixture. Stuff the squid with this mixture, sewing the opening with kitchen thread.
Peel the tomatoes by blanching them in hot water, remove the seeds and chop. Heat a few spoonfuls of oil and flavour with a crushed garlic clove; as soon as the garlic begins to colour, remove it and add the tomatoes.
When the sauce begins to simmer, add the squid, a pinch of salt and one of ground hot red pepper; cover and simmer for 30-40 minutes, then drain the fish and keep it warm together with a few spoonfuls of the sauce.
Boil the bucatini in salted water and drain when al dente. Mix into the sauce in the pot, sprinkle with chopped parsley and drizzle with oil.
Garnish with the sliced, stuffed squid and the remaining sauce.

BUCATINI
WITH FRIED FISH

◆

400 g bucatini, 400 g small frying fish, 1 ripe and firm tomato, 3 garlic cloves, 1 small bunch parsley, 1 handful basil leaves, 1 handful celery leaves, white flour, extra-virgin olive oil, salt and pepper.

Blanch the tomato in boiling water so it can be skinned easily. Cut it into wedges, discard the seeds, sprinkle with salt and leave to drain for a few minutes. Chop coarsely and mix with the peeled, halved garlic cloves in a large bowl. Leave to rest for about 30 minutes.
Remove the garlic, drizzle with oil, season with salt and pepper, and sprinkle with finely chopped herbs. Wash and dry the fish carefully, roll in the flour, and fry in hot oil.

In the meantime, cook the bucatini in salted water, drain, mix with the seasoned tomato and garnish with the fried fish.

BUCATINI WITH SARDINES AND FENNEL

◆

400 g bucatini, 800 g sardines, 150 g fennel hearts, 2 cloves garlic, 2 teaspoons raisins, 2 teaspoons pine-nuts, 1 sprig parsley, breadcrumbs, extra-virgin olive oil, salt, ground hot red pepper.

Clean the sardines, rinse and leave to dry on a dishcloth. Blanch the fennel hearts in boiling salted water for a few minutes, drain and cut into wedges. Soak the raisins in lukewarm water for fifteen minutes. Crush the garlic and sauté in a few tablespoons of oil. As soon as the garlic begins to brown, remove it and add the sardines to the oil. Cook them on both sides for a few minutes. Add the raisins (drained), the pine-nuts, 2 teaspoons of chopped parsley, 1 teaspoon of breadcrumbs, a pinch of salt and one of ground hot red pepper. Cook the

sauce over moderate heat, shaking the pan gently by the handle every now and then so as not to break the sardines. Just before turning off the heat, remove the sardines and set them aside.

Boil the bucatini and when al dente, drain and stir into the sauce. Serve garnished with the whole sardines and a sprinkling of fresh chopped parsley.

NESTS OF SPAGHETTI AND SEAFOOD

◆

250 g larger-sized spaghetti, 300 g shelled prawns, 16 scallops, 2 cloves garlic, 1 small bunch parsley, 1 glass dry white wine, extra-virgin olive oil, salt and pepper.

Scrub the scallop shells, place them in a large pot with a clove of garlic and half a glass of wine, cover and allow them to open over moderate heat. Turn off the heat, remove the scallops, strain the liquid and set it aside. Remove them from the shell, discard the inedible parts, separate the roe from the white flesh and set the roe aside.

In a large pot, heat 2-3 tablespoons of oil with a clove of garlic. Remove the garlic as soon as it starts to turn golden. Add the sliced scallops and sauté for a couple of minutes over high heat. Add the prawns and sauté for two more minutes. Add half a glass of wine and let it evaporate.

Add a little of the scallops' cooking juice, season with plenty of pepper and a little salt, and cook for another

4-5 minutes. The sauce should be allowed to dry almost completely. Add the chopped parsley, cover and keep warm. Cook the spaghetti in salted water, drain when al dente, spread out on the plate and drizzle with oil to keep it from sticking.

Divide the spaghetti into eight portions and place the first portion in a wire ladle to form a nest.

Heat abundant oil in a deep pot, dip the nest into the oil and golden-fry it. Drain well, remove the pasta from the scoop and keep warm. Repeat with the other portions of spaghetti.

Arrange the nests of pasta on a serving dish. Add the scallop roe to the seafood mixture, mix and fill each nest with the sauce.

FARFALLE
WITH SCALLOPS
AND ASPARAGUS

◆

350 g farfalle (butterfly-shaped pasta), 150 g asparagus, 150 g shelled scallops, 150 g single cream, 100 g porcini mushrooms, 1 shallot, 1 sprig parsley, 30 ml dry vermouth, butter, extra-virgin olive oil, salt and pepper.

Clean the asparagus by scraping the stems and cutting off the tough leathery parts at the bottom; rinse and cook in boiling water for a few minutes. Drain and cut into slices.

Clean the mushrooms with a cotton cloth and slice them, keeping the heads separate from the stems. Sauté the stems in three tablespoons of olive oil over

moderate heat for one minute, then add the tips. Sauté for a few minutes more, add salt and pepper, remove from the heat, and set aside. Clean and chop the shallot, then cook in 20 g of butter until transparent. Add the sliced scallops, season with salt and pepper and let brown. Add 30 g dry vermouth.

When the liquid has evaporated, add the mushrooms and asparagus. Continue cooking over medium-high heat, let the sauce reduce a little, then add the cream; lower the heat and season to taste. Cook the farfalle in salted water, drain when al dente, mix with the sauce and serve sprinkled with a spoonful of chopped parsley.

FETTUCCINE
WITH BAKED SOLE

◆

400 g fettuccine (recipe on page 133), 4-5 sole fillets (about 800 g), 150 g mussels, 150 g prawns, 150 g champignon mushrooms, 1/2 lemon, paprika, 2 egg yolks, 1.5 dl single cream, 1.5 dl dry white wine, 30 g butter, extra-virgin olive oil, salt and pepper.

Wash and shell the prawns. Clean the mussels, place them in a covered pan with one or two tablespoons of oil over moderate heat and allow them to open. Separate the mussels from the shell. Clean any grit or soil from the mushrooms with a damp cloth, slice them, and sauté together with the prawns and mussels in a few tablespoons of oil. Add salt and pepper and cook for a few minutes. Remove from the heat.

In an ovenproof dish, heat a few spoon-fuls of oil and brown the sole on both sides, add the wine and a pinch each of paprika, salt and pepper. Bake the fish until done in a hot oven (180 °C).

Remove from the oven, remove the fish and strain the cooking juices. Cook the strained liquid in a pan until it is reduced. Stirring constantly, add the cream and a little strained lemon juice, the egg yolks, the butter cut into pieces and some freshly ground pepper (one turn of the mill). Let thicken.

Cook the fettuccine in salted water, drain when al dente, drizzle with oil and transfer to an overproof dish. Lay the fish fillets over the pasta and add the mushroom and seafood sauce. Mix all together with the cream sauce.

In a hot oven, bake the dish au gratin at 200 °C. Serve piping hot.

FETTUCCINE
WITH CRAB

📷

400 g fettuccine (recipe on page 133), 4 crabs, 1 small onion, 1 clove garlic, 40 g wild fennel, 200 g ripe tomatoes, dry white wine, extra-virgin olive oil, salt.

The original recipe calls for 'gnac-chere', molluscs found off the Sardin-ian coast with a beautiful shell, which gives this dish its spectacular appear-ance. However, gnacchere taste almost exactly like crab-meat, which is more readily available. Crabmeat can thus be used without changing the taste of this recipe in any way.

Blanch the tomatoes in hot water for a few seconds, remove the skins and seeds and cut into cubes. Finely chop the on-ion and garlic.

Scoop out the crabmeat and cut it into pieces. Sauté the onion and garlic in the oil, add the wine and let it evaporate, then add the crab.

Cook for a few minutes over moder-ate heat, remove from the heat and add the tomatoes. In a pot with a lit-tle lightly salted water, boil the fennel for 10 minutes, add the pasta and cook together. The liquid should be almost entirely dried up.

Drain the pasta, mix into the sauce, salt to taste and add the oil. Mix carefully and serve.

FUSILLI
WITH SCAMPI
AND ZUCCHINI

◆

400 g fusilli, 450 g scampi, 350 g zucchini, 1 shallot, 1 sprig parsley, 1/2 litre of fish stock, extra-virgin olive oil, salt and pepper.

Cut the zucchini into julienne strips and clean the scampi carefully. Sauté the finely chopped shallot in a few ta-blespoons of oil; as soon as it becomes transparent, add the zucchini and the scampi.

Add salt and pepper and cook over low heat, adding a little fish stock. Boil the fusilli in abundant salted water and drain when al dente. Mix in the sauce, drizzle with oil and sprinkle with a handful of chopped parsley.

LINGUINE
AND SEAFOOD

◆

400 g linguine, 500 g mussels, 400 g clams, 500 g ripe and firm tomatoes, 3 cloves garlic, a few basil leaves, 2 sprigs oregano, extra-virgin olive oil, salt, ground hot red pepper.

Scrub the shells of the mussels and clams. Soak them in salted water for at least half an hour to get rid of any sand. Heat some oil over high heat, add one crushed garlic clove and fresh oregano to taste, add the shellfish and let the shells open. As they open, split the shells in two, discarding the empty half. When all have opened, turn off the heat, strain the cooking juices and set them aside. Peel the tomatoes by blanching them in hot water, remove the seeds and chop coarsely. Heat a few tablespoons of oil with the two remaining garlic cloves. Add the tomatoes and let them dry out for a few minutes over high heat, then lower the heat, add salt and a little ground hot red pepper.
Boil the linguine in abundant salted water, drain when al dente. Mix in the sauce and add the mussels and clams in the half-

shell, a mixture of chopped basil and oregano and a ladleful of strained juices from the shellfish. Mix carefully, transfer the pasta and sauce to a sheet of aluminum foil, close the foil over the pasta and pinch the edges together (don't let the foil stick to the food). Place in a very hot oven (220 °C) for about 5 minutes. Remove from the oven and transfer the 'package' to a serving dish. Open the aluminum foil to reveal the pasta.
The pasta can be served in one large portion or in several small ones, each wrapped individually in aluminum foil.

LINGUINE WITH SCAMPI
AND LEMON

◆

400 g linguine, 400 g scampi, 1 lemon, 1 clove garlic, 1 bunch parsley, ground hot red pepper, extra-virgin olive oil, salt.

To enjoy the flavour of this dish at its best, the sauce should be prepared at the last moment, while you are cooking the linguine. Clean and wash the scampi, then dry them and cut them in two lengthways.
Heat abundant oil in a large saucepan, flavouring it with the crushed garlic clove. As soon as the garlic begins to colour, remove it and add the scampi. Season with salt and a pinch of hot red pepper, and cook for about ten minutes, turning the shellfish from time to time. Cook the linguine in plenty of boiling salted water, draining them while still al dente, then pour

them into the saucepan with the scampi. Sprinkle with the juice of the lemon, thickly grated lemond rind, and a handful of finely-chopped parsley. Mix carefully, allowing the flavours to blend, and serve piping hot.

MALLOREDDUS WITH SWORDFISH SAUCE

◆

400 g malloreddus (recipe on page 134), 2 slices of swordfish, 500 g ripe tomatoes, 25 g salted capers, 1 small onion, 2 garlic cloves, 1 bay leaf, a few basil leaves, 1/2 glass of dry white wine, extra-virgin olive oil, salt and pepper.

This traditional Sardinian pasta goes well with fish sauce, but it is usually eaten dry and is therefore best when prepared a few days before.
Clean the swordfish and cut into cubes, around 2 cm square. Blanch the tomatoes in hot water, peel, remove the seeds and chop finely.
Sauté a mixture of chopped onion and garlic in a few tablespoons of oil. As soon as it is transparent, add the fish and, a few minutes later, the white wine. When the wine has almost evaporated, add the chopped tomatoes. Add salt, freshly ground pepper, the bay leaf, and the rinsed and dried capers. Simmer over moderate heat for about twenty minutes, sprinkle with some chopped basil and remove from the heat. Cook the pasta in abundant salted water, drain

when al dente and mix with half the sauce. Garnish with the remaining sauce and serve.

MALTAGLIATI WITH CALAMARI AND VEGETABLES

◆

400 g packet or home-made malta-gliati (recipe on page 138), 300 g squid, 3 sprigs black salsify, 200 g ripe tomatoes, 2 large potatoes, 1 clove garlic, 1 small bunch parsley, ground hot red pepper, extra-virgin olive oil, salt.

Make a dough for the maltagliati, using the basic recipe for tagliatelle. Cut the dough into strips measuring roughly 1.5 x 6-7 cm; precise measurements are not important. (The name of the pasta means 'cut badly'). Leave the strips to dry on a floured teacloth.
Blanch the tomatoes in hot water, remove the skin and seeds, and chop coarsely. Clean the squid, cut into strips and sauté in a few tablespoons of oil, then add the chopped tomatoes and continue to cook. A few minutes before removing from the heat, add salt, a little hot red pepper and a mixture of chopped parsley and garlic. Bring a pot of salted water to the boil and cook the potatoes, which have been cut into slices about 0.5 cm thick, and the black salsify, which has been cleaned and sliced. After 5 minutes, add the maltagliati. Drain the pasta and vegetables together and transfer to the pot with the sauce. Toss for a few seconds, mixing well. Remove from the heat, drizzle with oil and serve.

ORECCHIETTE
WITH SARDINES

◆

400 g orecchiette (recipe on page 135), 200 g sardines, 20 g pine-nuts, 1 ladle of tomato sauce, 1 anchovy fillet in oil, 1 clove garlic, 1 leek, 1 small bunch parsley, 1/4 teaspoon saffron, 1/2 hot red pepper, extra-virgin olive oil, pepper.

Clean the sardines, remove the bones and cut into slices. Prepare a mixture of chopped leek, garlic, hot red pepper, a little parsley and the anchovy fillet and sauté it in oil. Add the sardines and cook until golden brown. Add the pine-nuts, tomato sauce and saffron. Continue to cook over low heat.

Cook the pasta, drain and transfer to the pot with the sauce. Sauté for a few minutes. Remove from the heat, garnish with the chopped parsley and serve immediately.

PASTA
WITH TWAITE SHAD FILLETS

◆

400 g pasta (any short pasta will do), 8 twaite shad fillets in oil, 1 small onion, 2 cloves garlic, 300 g fresh tomato sauce, 1 small bunch parsley, about ten black olives, 4 teaspoons capers, paprika, extra-virgin olive oil, butter, salt.

Heat some oil and about a tablespoon of butter; add the chopped onion and the whole cloves of garlic, the twaite shad fillets, chopped capers, pitted olives and the fresh tomato sauce.

Cook for about ten minutes, then add the salt, chopped parsley and a pinch of paprika. In a deep pot, boil the pasta in salted water, drain when al dente, mix with the sauce and serve.

PASTA
WITH SARDINES,
SICILIAN STYLE

◆

400 g maccheroncini, 350 g fresh sardines, 200 g wild fennel, 80 g anchovies in oil, 30 g pine nuts, 30 g raisins, 2 cloves of garlic, 3 1/2 tablespoons extra-virgin olive oil, 2 teaspoons chopped parsley, 2 teaspoons breadcrumbs, saffron, ground hot red pepper, salt and pepper.

Clean the sardines, wash and leave to dry on a tea-cloth. Cook the fennel for a few minutes in a little salted water; drain and dice. Soak the raisins in luke-warm water for 15 minutes.

Crush the garlic and sauté in a few tablespoons of oil over low heat. As soon as the garlic begins to colour, remove and add the sardines. Brown on both sides. Add the fennel, the drained raisins, pine nuts, chopped parsley, breadcrumbs, salt and hot red pepper.

Continue cooking, gently shaking the pot so as to shift the sauce without breaking the fish; when the sardines are done, remove from the pot and set aside. Add the anchovies to the pan with a pinch of saffron diluted in a little water. Cook for a few minutes until the anchovies melt.

Boil the maccheroncini in salted water (preferably the water used to cook the fennel). Drain when al dente.

Place layers of pasta in an oven dish,

alternating with the sauce and the sardines. Finish with a layer of pasta and a layer of sauce. Bake in the oven at 200 °C for about 20 minutes. Serve piping hot.

PENNE WITH CAVIAR AND VODKA

◆

400 g penne, 1 small jar caviar, 2-3 small glasses vodka, 1 glass single cream, butter, salt and pepper.

In a pot, melt a heaping tablespoon of butter in the vodka and cook until it evaporates a little. Add the caviar, cream, salt and pepper; remove from the heat as soon as the sauce is warm. In the meantime, cook the penne in abundant salted water, drain when al dente. Flavour with the vodka and caviar sauce, mixing carefully so as not to break the fish eggs.

PENNE WITH SALMON AND WALNUTS

◆

400 g penne, 200 g sliced smoked salmon, 50 g peeled pistachios, 10 walnuts, 1 small onion, 1 egg yolk, cognac, extra-virgin olive oil, salt, freshly-ground pepper.

Chop the onion finely, chop the walnuts and pistachios more coarsely, then sauté all together in a large saucepan with a few spoonfuls of oil. After a few minutes, pour in a little cognac and let it evaporate, then add the

salmon cut into small strips, along with a twist of freshly-ground pepper. Let the flavours blend for a few moments, then remove from the heat. In a large serving bowl, mix the egg yolk with a few spoonfuls of oil and a pinch of salt. Pour the pasta (boiled, and drained while still al dente) into the bowl, pour the salmon sauce over it, and mix all the ingredients thoroughly before serving.

In a variation of this recipe, a quarter litre of fresh table cream is used instead of the egg yolk.

PENNE AND PRAWNS IN FOIL

◆

400 g penne, 150 g shelled prawns, 100 g smoked ham in one slice, 150 g fresh hulled peas, 1 small onion, dry white wine, extra-virgin olive oil, salt and pepper.

Cut the ham into cubes. Wash the prawns and sauté them in a few spoonfuls of oil. Add the wine, then the finely chopped onion, the cubed ham and the peas. Season with salt and pepper and simmer, adding a ladleful of hot water if necessary. Boil the pasta in salted water and drain when al dente. Drizzle with oil and add to the pan containing the peas, ham and prawns. Transfer to a sheet of aluminum foil and close the foil. Bake in a hot oven (180 °C) for about ten minutes. Serve with the foil opened to reveal the pasta.

This pasta can be served as one large dish or several small ones, each individually wrapped in foil.

SPAGHETTI
WITH SQUID INK

◆

400 g spaghetti, 400 g baby squid, a few ink sacs, 5 ripe tomatoes (optional), 1 clove garlic, 1 sprig parsley, extra-virgin olive oil, salt, ground hot red pepper.

Clean the squid, removing the bones, eyes and ink sacs. Be careful not to break the sacs, since they will be used later. Wash the squid carefully, then chop it coarsely. Sauté some crushed garlic in a few spoonfuls of oil, add the pieces of squid and a ladleful of warm water. Simmer for 15 minutes. Peel the tomatoes and remove the seeds. Chop roughly and add to the squid. When the sauce has thickened, break the ink sacs into the pot along with a handful of chopped parsley, salt and hot red pepper. Let the flavours blend. Cook the spaghetti in salted water, drain when al dente and add to the

sauce. This dish can also be made without the tomatoes, using instead some white wine and a few ladles of warm stock to flavour the squid.

SPAGHETTI ALLA CHITARRA
WITH RAZOR CLAMS

◆

500 g spaghetti alla chitarra (recipe on page 136), 1 kg razor clams (or clams, date mussels, or Venus clams), 800 g ripe tomatoes, 3 cloves garlic, a small bunch of parsley, 1/2 glass dry white wine, extra-virgin olive oil, salt, 1 fresh hot red pepper.

Wash the razor clams, put them in a pan with the wine over high heat and let them open. Separate the molluscs from the shell (keep some whole for decoration) and strain the liquid. Sauté some crushed garlic and chopped hot red pepper in a few tablespoons of oil, add the tomatoes (peeled, with their seeds removed and coarsely chopped) and salt, and cook for about 15 minutes. Dilute the sauce with the cooking liquid of the razor clams, cook another 10 minutes and add the molluscs, which have been cut into small pieces. Continue to simmer for another 5 minutes. In the meantime, boil the spaghetti in abundant salted water and drain when al dente. Remove the sauce from the heat, mix in the spaghetti and serve with chopped parsley and garnished with the whole razor clams. This recipe works just as well with any available mixture of shellfish.

SPAGHETTI WITH LOBSTER

◆

400 g spaghetti, 1 medium-sized lobster, 250 g tomato purée, 2 cloves garlic, 1 small bunch parsley, extra-virgin olive oil, salt, freshly ground pepper.

Boil the lobster for a few minutes in salted water, drain, remove the shell and cut the meat into pieces. In a pot sauté the garlic clove with oil, add the lobster and cook for a few minutes before adding the tomato purée, chopped parsley and salt. Simmer over low heat. In the meantime, boil the pasta in abundant salted water, drain when al dente and serve with the lobster sauce and some freshly ground pepper.

SPAGHETTI AND SEAFOOD BAKED IN FOIL

◆

400 g spaghetti, 500 g shellfish (mussels and clams), 200 g squid, 4 small scampi, 4 prawns, 300 g ripe and mature tomatoes, basil, a small onion, dry white wine, extra-virgin olive oil, salt, 1 small hot red pepper.

Clean the various types of fish. Let the mussels and clams open over low heat in a pot with half a glass of white wine. As they open, separate the molluscs

from the shell (leaving a few whole as garnish).

Strain the cooking juices and set aside. Blanch the tomatoes in hot water, peel them, remove the seeds and chop coarsely. In a large pot, wilt the finely chopped onion in a few tablespoons of oil; when the onion is transparent, add the tomatoes. Add the chopped squid, cook for 10 minutes, then add the scampi and prawns. Add the liquid from the mussels and clams, the hot red pepper, season to taste, and simmer for about 10 minutes. Add the mussels and clams to the sauce, let the flavours blend, and remove from the heat.

Boil the spaghetti in abundant salted water, drain when al dente, mix carefully with the sauce and sprinkle with chopped basil. Place the spaghetti on the foil, well covered by the scampi and whole prawns. Pinch the edges of the foil together; do not let the foil stick to the pasta. Bake in a hot oven (180 °C) for 5 minutes.

Serve with the foil open. This dish can be served as one large portion or several small individually wrapped portions.

SPAGHETTI
WITH ANCHOVIES
AND TRUFFLES

◆

400 g spaghetti, 4 medium-sized black truffles, 4 salted anchovies, 1 clove garlic, extra-virgin olive oil, salt, white pepper.

Wash the anchovies carefully under running water and remove the bones. Clean the truffles, removing the soil completely, and pound in a mortar. Heat a little oil in a pot, add the anchovies and let them melt, add the crushed garlic and the truffles, salt and pepper. Do not fry the mixture.
In the meantime, bring a pot of salted water to the boil, add the spaghetti, cook and drain when al dente. Dress with the anchovy and truffle sauce and serve.

SPAGHETTI
WITH FRESH
ANCHOVIES

◆

400 g spaghetti, 250 g fresh anchovies, 2 cloves garlic, 1/2 lemon, 1 small bunch parsley, 40 g breadcrumbs, extra-virgin olive oil, salt, ground hot red pepper.

This sauce can be prepared very quickly and the fish is easily cleaned. Discarding the heads, tails and backbones, then wash the anchovies carefully in running water; dry and place in a pan with the chopped garlic and parsley, breadcrumbs and oil.
Cook over high heat for a few minutes,

stirring until the anchovies are soft and the breadcrumbs are golden. Add salt and ground hot red pepper. Drain the pasta when al dente, mix with the sauce and drizzle with lemon juice before serving.

SPAGHETTI
WITH CLAMS

📷

400 g spaghetti, 1 kg clams, 2 cloves garlic, a small bunch parsley, dry white wine (optional), extra-virgin olive oil, salt, 1 hot red pepper.

Clean the shellfish under cold running water, then soak in salted water for half an hour to get rid of any sand. This is very important and should be done with care, as the sauce will not be strained.
In a large pan, heat several tablespoons of oil, 1 chopped garlic clove, the hot red pepper and a little wine if desired. Add the clams, cover the pan and let the clams open.
In the meantime cook the spaghetti in salted water, drain when al dente and transfer to the pan with the clams. Mix over low heat and sprinkle with a mixture of chopped garlic and parsley. Remove from the heat and serve.

SPAGHETTI
WITH BABY EELS

◆

400 g spaghetti, 200 g fresh baby eels, 1 clove garlic, 1 sprig sage, 2 1/2 tablespoons of tomato sauce, extra-virgin olive oil, salt.

Wash the eels thoroughly. In a pot, heat a few tablespoons of oil and sauté the sage leaves. Add the eels.

Do this quickly, being ready with the lid in case the heat makes the eels jump out of the pot.

Lower the heat and simmer for about 10 minutes.

Boil the spaghetti in salted water, drain when al dente, transfer to the pot with the eels and stir in the tomato sauce. Mix well, season to taste, and serve.

SPAGHETTI WITH CLAMS IN TOMATO SAUCE

◆

400 g spaghetti, 500 g clams, 500 g tomato pulp, 2 cloves garlic, a small bunch parsley, 1/2 glass of extra-virgin olive oil, salt, 1 small hot red pepper.

Wash the clams carefully and leave for half an hour in salted water to remove any sand.

In a large pan, heat the oil with the garlic cloves and as soon as they begin to colour, remove them and add the tomato pulp.

Cook a few minutes over high heat, then lower the heat, add salt and the hot red pepper. When the sauce has thickened, add the clams.

Boil the spaghetti in plenty of salted water, drain when al dente and mix with the clam sauce and a sprinkle of chopped parsley.

Stir over the heat for a few minutes to let the flavours blend.

BLACK TAGLIATELLE WITH KING PRAWNS

400 g black tagliatelle (recipe on page 138), 8 king prawns, 1 clove garlic, 1 small bunch parsley, 1 glass dry white wine, extra-virgin olive oil, salt.

Prepare the pasta dough and colour it as described on page 133. Sauté the shelled prawns in oil, flavouring with chopped parsley, garlic and a pinch of salt. Add the white wine and cook over high heat for three minutes.

Boil the pasta in abundant salted water, drain when al dente and transfer to the pan with the sauce.

Mix carefully for a few minutes and remove from the heat. Serve piping hot and garnish with the remaining finely chopped parsley.

TAGLIATELLE WITH ANCHOVIES AND BREADCRUMBS

◆

400 g tagliatelle (recipe on page 138), 6 salted anchovies, 25 g pine-nuts, 3 cloves garlic, parsley, 2 1/2 heaping tablespoons stale breadcrumbs, 1/2 glass extra-virgin olive oil, salt, ground hot red pepper.

Clean the salt and bones from the anchovies, using a knife and a damp cloth. Heat some oil in a pan, flavour with the crushed garlic (removing as soon as it begins to colour) and a little ground hot red pepper. Add the anchovies and cook with some chopped parsley and pine-nuts.

In a non-stick saucepan, toast the breadcrumbs until golden brown but not dark, turning them with a spoon. Boil the pasta in abundant salted water and drain when al dente.

Mix with the anchovies and half of the toasted breadcrumbs. Transfer to a serving dish.

Serve the remaining breadcrumbs on the side, to be sprinkled over the individual portions like grated Parmesan.

maining butter in a pan with a clove of garlic (remove as soon as it begins to colour) and sauté the scallops. After a few minutes, add the vermouth and let it evaporate.

Remove from the heat, season to taste, sprinkle with chopped parsley and keep warm.

Boil the tagliatelle and drain when al dente. Mix the pasta into the butter sauce and garnish with the scallops.

TAGLIATELLE WITH SCALLOPS

◆

400 g black tagliatelle (recipe on page 138), 12 scallops, 1 shallot, 1 clove garlic, 1 small bunch parsley, 2 dl fish stock, 1 dl single cream, 1/2 glass of dry vermouth, 1 dl dry white wine, 120 g butter, salt and pepper.

Prepare the pasta dough and colour it as specified on page 133. Chop the shallot finely and wilt it over heat with the wine and fish stock.

Cook until the liquid is reduced by half, add the cream and thicken the sauce over low heat, stirring constantly.

Add 100 g butter, which has been softened at room temperature and cut into small pieces. Season with salt and pepper. Remove the sauce from the heat but keep it warm.

Open the scallops, separate the fish from the shells, clean and discard the inedible parts, and separate the meat from the roe. Heat the re-

TAGLIATELLE WITH TROUT

◆

400 g tagliatelle (recipe on page 138), 250 g trout fillets, 4 peeled tomatoes, 3 zucchini, 1 small onion, dry white wine, extra-virgin olive oil, salt and pepper.

Sauté the finely chopped onion in a little olive oil, add the trout fillets cut into strips, and cover with white wine. Let the wine evaporate, then add the tomatoes cut into pieces and the zucchini sliced in thin disks.

Season with salt and pepper and continue

to simmer over low heat. In the meantime, boil the tagliatelle in abundant salted water, drain when al dente and serve mixed with the trout.

TAGLIOLINI WITH CAVIAR

◆

400 g tagliolini (recipe on page 138), 1 small jar caviar or lumpfish roe, juice of 1 lemon, 1.5 dl single cream, 80 g butter, freshly ground pepper.

Place the caviar in a bowl and add a few drops of lemon juice. Soften the butter at room temperature, chop into small pieces and mix in a large serving bowl with the cream, which has been slightly warmed.
Boil the tagliolini and drain when al dente. Transfer to the serving dish and mix carefully with the butter and cream; stir in the caviar and some freshly ground pepper.

TAGLIOLINI WITH SALMON

◆

400 g tagliolini (recipe on page 138), 150 g smoked salmon, 1 clove garlic, 1 lemon, 1 cup of fresh single cream, 30 g butter, salt, freshly ground white pepper.

Heat the butter in a saucepan and flavour with the garlic clove; transfer to a large pot and remove the garlic. Heat the pot, add the cream, the chopped salmon, a little grated lemon rind (the yellow part only), a pinch of salt, and

stir gently. In the meantime, boil the tagliolini in salted water, drain when al dente and transfer to the pot with the salmon sauce.
Stir for a few minutes over the heat, add a little more butter if necessary and some freshly ground pepper.

TAGLIOLINI WITH BOTTARGA

◆

400 g tagliolini (recipe on page 138), 3 slices of bottarga, 1/2 clove garlic, 1 small bunch parsley, the juice of 1/2 lemon, extra-virgin olive oil, pepper.

Bottarga is salted mullet roe and looks like a kind of hard greyish-brown salami. It can be sliced thin and used to prepare canapés, or grated like Parmesan over a plate of pasta.
The following recipe suggests another way to use bottarga as a garnish for pasta. Boil the pasta in abundant salted water. In the meantime, sauté the bottarga in 2 tablespoons of oil and a little of the pasta water.
As soon as the bottarga has melted, add the lemon juice. Drain the tagliolini when al dente and mix into the bottarga, sprinkle with pepper, and a mixture of chopped parsley and garlic.

TROFIE
WITH SQUID

◆

400 g trofie (recipe on page 136), 400 g squid, 1 cup of tomato sauce, 1 sprig basil, 1 small onion, 1 clove garlic, 1 glass dry white wine, 1/2 hot red pepper, extra-virgin olive oil, salt.

Skin and remove the bone from the squid, wash in running water, and re-move the tentacles. Cut the body into strips. Sauté a mixture of sliced onion, garlic and crushed hot red pepper in oil. Add the strips of squid and the tenta-cles, which have been diced and salted. Add the white wine; when it has evap-orated, add the tomato sauce. Simmer over low heat.
Cook the pasta in abundant salted water, drain, and transfer to the pan with the sauce. Toss for a couple of minutes, then remove from the heat. Sprinkle with the chopped fresh basil and serve.

TROFIE
WITH ANCHOVY SAUCE

◆

400 g trofie (recipe on page 136), 4 anchovy fil-lets in oil, 1 white onion, 1 glass dry white wine, 1 sprig basil, 1 ripe tomato, 1/2 hot red pepper, extra-virgin olive oil.

Mash the anchovies with a fork. Chop the on-ion and the hot red pepper and sauté them in the oil. Add the anchovies and the white wine. Let it

evaporate. Blanch the tomatoes in hot, lightly salted water, peel them, remove their seeds, and cut them into strips. Cook the pasta and drain when al dente. Transfer to a large serving bowl. Add the anchovies and raw tomatoes, a little more extra-virgin olive oil, some basil leaves, and serve.

VERMICELLI
WITH SEAFOOD

◆

400 g vermicelli, 500 g mussels and clams, 200 g fresh lobster meat, 4-5 small scampi, 4-5 king prawns, 500 g ripe and firm tomatoes, 1 small onion, 1 handful basil leaves, 1/2 glass dry white wine, extra-virgin olive oil, salt, ground hot red pepper.

Clean the various types of seafood. Rinse and soak them in salted water to elimi-nate any sandy residue. Do not remove the shells. Heat the white wine in a pot and add the mussels and clams; as they open, remove the molluscs from the shell (leave a few as garnish). Strain the liquid in the pot and set aside. Blanch the tomatoes in hot water, peel them, remove the seeds and chop coarsely.
In a large pot, sauté the finely chopped onion in a few ta-blespoons of oil. Add the toma-toes and cook them a few minutes, then add the scampi

and prawns. After a few minutes, add the lobster meat cut into slices. Add the liquid from the mussels and clams, add salt, and flavour with hot red pepper.

Simmer for 10 minutes, then add the clams and mussels; let the flavours blend and remove from the heat. In the meantime, boil the vermicelli in abundant salted water; drain when al dente and gently stir into the sauce, adding a sprinkling of fresh basil.

You can also serve the vermicelli baked in foil. In this case, do not allow the pasta to dry in the sauce.

After mixing it with the fish, place it on a sheet of aluminum foil, making sure the pasta is well covered by the scampi and whole prawns.

Close the foil, pinching it round the edges but leaving a little space between the food and the foil. Bake in a hot oven (180 °C) for about five minutes.

Serve with the foil open. You can make one large portion or several small ones individually wrapped in foil.

VERMICELLI WITH RAZOR CLAMS

◆

400 g vermicelli, 1 kg razor clams, 800 g ripe tomatoes, 3 cloves garlic, 1 small bunch parsley, dry white wine, extra-virgin olive oil, salt, ground hot red pepper.

Wash the razor clams well and let them open in a pan with a little oil and wine over high heat.

Separate the molluscs from the shells (keeping some to one side) and strain the liquid in the pot.

Heat several tablespoons of oil in a pan, add a mixture of crushed garlic and ground hot red pepper, add the tomatoes (previously peeled, seeded and coarsely chopped), and cook for 15 minutes.

Dilute the sauce with the razor clam cooking juices, simmer for 10 minutes, then add the shellfish cut into pieces. Simmer 5 minutes more before removing from the heat.

Cook the vermicelli in salted water, drain when al dente and mix with the sauce. Sprinkle with chopped parsley, mix well, garnish with the whole shellfish.

The recipe can be used with all kinds of shellfish (clams, etc,).

Pasta,
vegetables and cheese

BIGOLI
ALLA PUTTANESCA
◆

400 g bigoli (recipe on page 137), 500 g tomato pulp, 1 1/2 tablespoons salted capers, 100 g black olives, 2 cloves garlic, 1 small bunch parsley, 2 salted anchovies, extra-virgin olive oil, salt, ground hot red pepper.

Rinse the capers in running water, pit the olives, and clean the salt and bones from the anchovies. Heat some oil in a pan, add the tomatoes, capers, olives and anchovies.

Cook over high heat for 10-15 minutes, stirring frequently. Just before removing from the heat, check the seasoning, add a little hot red pepper and sprinkle with finely chopped parsley.

Boil the bigoli in abundant salted water, drain when al dente, and mix well with the sauce before serving.

BIGOLI
WITH FENNEL
◆

400 g bigoli (recipe on page 137), 150 g tomato purée, 2 fennel hearts, 1 onion, 1 bunch parsley, grated Parmesan cheese, extra-virgin olive oil, salt.

Wash the fennel, cut into quarters and blanch in boiling, salted water. Chop the onion and parsley, and sauté in a little oil over low heat. As soon as the onion is transparent, add the chopped

fennel and cook for 10 minutes. Add the tomato purée, a pinch of salt and continue to cook with the lid on until the fennel is tender and well blended into the sauce.

Cook the bigoli in salted water, drain when al dente, and transfer to a large serving bowl. Mix in the sauce, drizzle with oil, and sprinkle with Parmesan.

BUCATINI
ALLA BOSCAIOLA
◆

400 g bucatini, 500 g fresh mushrooms, 300 g tomato pulp, 1 clove garlic, 1 small bunch parsley, 2 teaspoons pine-nuts, 70 g speck cut into thick slices, 1/2 glass of dry white wine, extra-virgin olive oil, salt and pepper.

How you clean the mushrooms will depend on the kind you use. Remove the soil from the heads and stems with a damp cloth. If the mushrooms are large, slice them and sauté the slices in a pot with oil and chopped garlic. Let them brown, add the wine, and as soon as it has evaporated, add the tomato pulp and season with salt and pepper. Lower the heat and simmer, covered for about 15 minutes.

In the meantime, cut the speck into cubes and brown in a little oil with the pine-nuts and chopped parsley. Add the speck to the mushrooms, stirring gently to let the flavours blend. Mix in the pasta, which has been cooked until al dente and then drained.

BUCATINI WITH ONIONS
◆

400 g bucatini, 3 large onions, thyme, hot red pepper, grated Parmesan cheese, extra-virgin olive oil, salt.

Slice the onion and stew it in oil over low heat, stirring to keep it from sticking. When the onion is almost done, add a pinch of thyme, one of ground hot red pepper and one of salt.
Boil the pasta in abundant salted water, drain when al dente and dress with the sauce and a little oil.

CAVATIEDDI WITH ROCKET AND TOMATOES
◆

400 g cavatieddi (recipe on page 133), 500 g tomato pulp, 300 g rocket, 1 clove garlic, extra-virgin olive oil, mature ricotta, salt, hot red pepper.

Heat the oil and flavour with the crushed garlic cloves. Add the tomato pulp and simmer over low heat for about 15 minutes, stirring from time to time.
Wash the rocket and parboil it in boiling salted water for a few minutes. Use the same water to cook the cavatieddi.

Drain when al dente and transfer to the pan with the sauce. Stir in the chopped rocket, a sprinkling of grated ricotta and a pinch of hot red pepper. Mix well and serve.

FARFALLE WITH LEMON
◆

400 g farfalle (butterfly-shaped pasta), the juice of one and a half lemons (or one very juicy lemon), 1 bunch basil and chives, 1 glass cream, 50 g butter, salt and pepper.

This is an extremely tasty dish, quick and easy to make. Cut the butter into pieces and let it soften at room temperature. In a large serving dish, blend the butter into the lemon juice, working it to form a soft, creamy sauce. Flavour with salt, pepper and finely chopped aromatic herbs.
Boil the farfalle in plenty of salted water and drain when al dente. Transfer to the serving dish with the lemon-butter sauce and mix carefully before serving.

FARFALLE WITH CHEESE AND MUSHROOMS
◆

400 g farfalle, 100 g Fontina cheese, 50 g grated Parmesan cheese, 50 g grated Gruyère, 250 g fresh mushrooms, 25 g dried mushrooms, 2 shallots, 4 ripe and firm tomatoes, 1 small bunch parsley, 2 teaspoons cream, white wine, extra-virgin olive oil, salt and pepper.

Soak the dried mushrooms. Clean the fresh ones carefully with a damp cloth,

and slice.
Dice the shallots and wilt them in a pan with oil; as they begin to colour, add the fresh mushrooms and sauté for a few minutes. Add a little wine. As soon as it evaporates, add the chopped dried mushrooms and the strained water used to soak them. Blanch the tomatoes in hot water, peel them, remove the seeds and chop them; add to the mushrooms, along with salt and pepper. Continue to stir, cooking over moderate heat for around 30 minutes. If necessary, dilute with a little stock or hot salted water. In a large bowl, mix the grated cheeses and the Fontina cut into little cubes with the cream, and about 10 minutes before turning off the heat, add them to the mushrooms.
In the meantime, boil the pasta in plenty of salted water, drain when al dente and mix into the sauce. Sprinkle with a little finely chopped parsley and stir over the heat for a few minutes more before serving.

FARFALLE WITH PEPPERS
◆

400 g farfalle, 40 g red and yellow peppers, 400 g ripe and firm tomatoes, 2 cloves garlic, 50 g salted capers, a few leaves of basil, extra-virgin olive oil, salt, ground hot red pepper.

Clean the peppers, removing the seeds and filaments. Place them on an oiled tray in a hot oven to wilt, then remove the scorched outer film. Cut the peppers into strips, reserving any cooking liquid. Heat a few tablespoons of oil with the crushed garlic; as soon as it begins to brown, remove it and add the peppers with their sauce. Cook for a few minutes, then add the tomatoes (first peel them, remove the seeds and chop coarsely). After about ten minutes over high heat, add the capers, which have been rinsed under running water and then dried. Add salt, and a minute or two before turning off the heat, a pinch of hot red pepper and some crushed basil leaves. Boil the farfalle in plenty of salted water, drain, and serve with the sauce.

FUSILLI WITH FOUR CHEESES
◆

400 g fusilli (curly pasta), 100 g sweet Gorgonzola, 100 g Fontina, 100 g Gruyère, 100 g Taleggio, milk, 1/2 glass cream, grated Parmesan cheese, salt and pepper.

In a small non-stick saucepan, melt the Gorgonzola, Fontina, Taleggio and Gruyère cut into small cubes together with a little milk. Stir constantly over low heat. Dilute the sauce with cream and flavour with salt, Parmesan and freshly ground pepper. Stir constantly to form a fluid, creamy sauce.
In the meantime, cook the pasta, drain when al dente and mix into the melted cheese. Serve with grated Parmesan.

FUSILLI
WITH BROAD BEANS

◆

400 g fusilli, 400 g fresh broad beans, 400 g ripe and firm tomatoes, 2 cloves garlic, a few basil leaves, extra-virgin olive oil, salt, ground hot red pepper.

Blanch the tomatoes in hot water, peel them, remove the seeds and chop. Sauté the chopped garlic in a pan, in a few tablespoons of oil. Clean the broad beans, discarding the black eye, then put them in the pan with the garlic. Let the flavours blend, then add the chopped tomatoes, salt, and a pinch of hot red pepper. Simmer over moderate heat, adding hot water if needed and crushed basil at the end. Boil the pasta in abundant salted water, drain when al dente, and add to the broad bean sauce.

FUSILLI WITH ENDIVE
AND POMEGRANATE

◆

400 g fusilli, 400 g endives, 2 pomegranates, 150 g ricotta, extra-virgin olive oil, salt and pepper.

Clean the endive and cut into strips. Boil in salted water with the pasta. Meanwhile, in a warmed dish, mix the ricotta with two spoonfuls of hot water from the pasta pot. Season with salt and pepper, and blend the pomegranate seeds into the mixture. Drain the pasta and endives and transfer to the serving bowl, mixing carefully with the ricotta and pomegranate. Drizzle with the oil.

LINGUINE
WITH SWEETENED
CAULIFLOWER

📷

400 g linguine, 1 onion, 1 medium-sized cauliflower, 80 g raisins, 80 g pine-nuts, salt and pepper, extra-virgin olive oil, grated Parmesan cheese (optional).

Soak the raisins in lukewarm water. In the meantime, clean the cauliflower, boil in a little salted water, drain while still very firm and cut into small pieces. In a pan, sauté the chopped onion in a little oil for a few minutes, then add the cauliflower and pine-nuts.
Drain the raisins and squeeze out the moisture. Add them, together with a little of the water they have soaked in, to the cauliflower and onion. Add a pinch of salt and one of pepper, and simmer over moderate heat.
Boil the pasta in plenty of salted water and when al dente, drain and transfer to a large serving bowl with half of the sauce. Bring to the table and drizzle the individual portions with the remaining sauce. Serve grated Parmesan on the side.

MACCHERONCINI PRIMAVERA

◆

400 g small whole-wheat maccheroncini, 1 kg asparagus, 300 g fresh ricotta cheese, 2 eggs, a little milk, 100 g grated Parmesan cheese, extra-virgin olive oil, salt, hot red pepper.

Clean the asparagus thoroughly and cook them for about 5 minutes in salted, boiling water. Drain them thoroughly, then cut into pieces, discarding the woody parts. Place them into a large saucepan with a few tablespoons of oil and sauté lightly.

In a bowl, blend the ricotta with a few spoonfuls of milk, a pinch of salt, and one of hot red pepper, beating to form a smooth, soft paste.

To cook the pasta, bring to the boil a large pot with the asparagus cooking water, adding more water if required. Pour in the maccheroncini, cook, and drain while still al dente.

Oil an ovenproof dish. Place in it a first layer of pasta, covering it with grated Parmesan cheese and a trickle of oil. Sprinkle half the asparagus over it and spread with half the ricotta cream. Repeat the layers of maccheroncini, asparagus and ricotta, finishing with a layer of maccheroncini. Pour over it the eggs, beaten with a pinch of salt, a pinch of hot red pepper, and a couple of spoons of grated Parmesan. Brown in the oven about half an hour before serving.

MALLOREDDUS WITH POTATOES

◆

400 g malloreddus (recipe on page 133), 400 g potatoes, 200 g onions, extra-virgin olive oil, grated pecorino, salt, freshly ground pepper.

The influence of Sardinia can be felt in both the pasta and this simple, tasty sauce. Remember that this type of pasta is better dry, so it can be made a couple of days in advance.

Clean the vegetables, cut the potatoes into cubes, and slice the onions. Bring a pot of salted water to the boil and add the potatoes.

After 15 minutes, add the pasta. In the meantime, heat some oil in a pan and sauté the finely chopped onion. Drain the potatoes and pasta when the latter is al dente.

Transfer to the pan with the onions, stir over moderate heat for a few seconds, add the grated pecorino and some freshly ground pepper. Remove from the heat and serve.

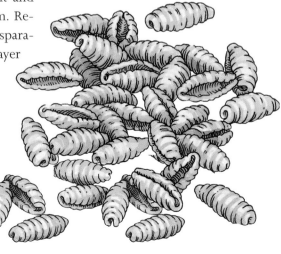

ORECCHIETTE WITH BROCCOLI

◆

400 g orecchiette (recipe on page 135), 300 g broccoli, 2 cloves garlic, 2 teaspoons raisins (optional), 2 salted anchovies, grated pecorino, extra-virgin olive oil, salt, ground hot red pepper.

Wash the broccoli carefully and cook it in abundant salted water. Drain while still firm but reserve the water to be used for cooking the pasta.
Soak the raisins in a small cup with lukewarm water.
Heat some olive oil and add the chopped garlic.
Clean the salt off the anchovies and blend them into the oil. Add the broccoli and let the sauce simmer (adding a little hot, salted water if necessary).
Shortly before removing from the heat, season to taste, and flavour with hot red pepper. Add the pine-nuts and raisins, which have been well-drained and squeezed dry.
Cook the orecchiette, drain when al dente, stir into the sauce and flavour with grated or finely cubed pecorino.

PANSOTTI WITH WALNUTS

◆

For the pasta: (recipe on page 138).
For the filling: 300 g ricotta, 500 g chard, 500 g a mix of cabbage, chard and parsley, 1 bunch of borage, 3 eggs, 50 g Parmesan cheese, nutmeg, salt.
For the sauce: walnuts, pine nuts, 1 clove garlic, extra-virgin olive oil.

Prepare the pasta as described in the recipe, roll out and cut into little 6-cm squares.
Make the filling: wash, boil and chop the vegetables. In a bowl, mix the ricotta, grated Parmesan, eggs, salt and some grated nutmeg; lastly, add the chopped vegetables.
Mix thoroughly to form a smooth stuffing. Drop a little of the mixture onto the centre of each pasta square. Fold the pasta over into a triangle, pressing the edges firmly together. Cook the pansotti in boiling, salted water. While they cook, prepare the sauce. Chop the walnuts, pine nuts and garlic, then pound all together in a mortar, adding enough oil to form a smooth, even sauce. Set aside to rest. Drain the pansotti when al dente and transfer to a warmed serving dish. Dress with the nut sauce and serve immediately.

PASTA
WITH RICOTTA

◆

400 g pasta (any short pasta will do), 250 g fresh ricotta, 100 g grated mature ricotta, lard, salt, ground hot red pepper.

Cook the pasta in plenty of salted water. In the meantime, prepare the sauce. Melt a little lard in a pot and stir in the fresh ricotta.

Drain the pasta when al dente and mix with the melted ricotta. Sprinkle with grated ricotta and a pinch of hot red pepper. Mix well before serving. You can personalize this recipe by adding aromatic herbs and other ingredients of your choice: oregano, ginger, or chopped black olives.

PASTA
WITH CARROTS

◆

400 g pasta (any short pasta will do), salt, 2 onions, 2 cloves garlic, about 10 medium-sized carrots, 2 celery stalks, 1 sprig rosemary, 2 teaspoons sesame seeds, extra-virgin olive oil, salt.

Clean the carrots thoroughly under running water, using a special brush; let them dry. Clean the celery.

Finely chop the onion and garlic, and place in a pan with the oil and rosemary. Sauté over high heat. Slice the carrots lengthwise and finely chop the celery. Add both to the pot, along with the sesame seeds and a pinch of salt. Cook for a few minutes, then lower the heat, cover and simmer for about 15 minutes, stirring occasionally to keep the mixture from sticking.

Boil the pasta in plenty of salted water; when al dente, drain and mix into the sauce. Toss over the heat for a few seconds. The success of this recipe depends largely on the carrots. They should be al dente, cooked through but still firm.

PASTA
WITH LENTILS

400 g whole-grain pasta (any short pasta will do), 200 g whole lentils, 1 carrot, 1 celery stick, 2 cloves garlic, 2 bay leaves, 1 bunch parsley, ground hot red pepper, extra-virgin olive oil, salt.

Soak the lentils for 12 hours. Drain, rinse, and cook in plenty of salted water along with the diced celery, diced carrot and bay leaves.

Cover the pot and simmer over moderate heat. When the lentils are almost done, add the pasta. Remove from the heat when the pasta is al dente. Transfer to a large serving bowl and dress with a sauce made of oil, chopped parsley, finely chopped garlic, and ground hot red pepper, all cooked for 15 minutes over moderate heat.

68

PASTA WITH ZUCCHINI PARMESAN

◆

400 g whole-grain pasta (any short type will do), 800 g zucchini, 1 kg ripe tomatoes, 150 g mozzarella, a few basil leaves, grated Parmesan cheese, extra-virgin olive oil, salt, ground hot red pepper.

Wash the zucchini and slice them lengthwise. Leave them for about an hour at room temperature or in the sun, then fry them in oil, letting them drain on paper towels.

Cook half of the sliced tomatoes in a pot with only a pinch of salt and a few basil leaves. In an oiled ovenproof dish, place a layer of tomato sauce, followed by a layer of zucchini, slices of mozzarella and grated Parmesan. Finish with a layer of zucchini and the last spoonfuls of sauce.

Place in a hot oven (180 °C) for about half an hour. In the meantime, blanch the remaining tomatoes in hot water, peel them and remove the seeds; cook in the same pot as before with oil, salt and hot red pepper. When done, add to the dish of Parmesan and zucchini. Mix and cook for about 10 minutes, adding if necessary, a few spoonfuls of hot water to keep it from sticking. Cook the pasta in salted water, drain and transfer to a serving dish. Cover with the sauce and add a few fresh basil leaves. Serve with grated Parmesan on the side.

PASTA WITH RICOTTA AND ARTICHOKES

📷

400 g pasta (any short pasta will do), 250 g ricotta, 4 artichokes, 1 shallot, 1 clove garlic, 1 lemon, 1 small bunch parsley, dry white wine, extra-virgin olive oil, grated Parmesan cheese, salt and pepper.

Pare the stem and remove the sharp tips from the outer leaves of the artichokes, cut into fine wedges, and soak in water diluted with lemon juice.

Finely chop the shallot and garlic, and sauté in several tablespoons of oil. Drain the artichokes and add to the pan, stirring constantly over high heat.

After a few minutes, lower the heat and add some white wine. Let it evaporate. Season with salt and pepper, cover and simmer about 20 minutes. If necessary, add a little hot, salted water.

Boil the pasta and drain it when al dente. Transfer to the pan with the sauce, add the crumbled ricotta, a few tablespoons of Parmesan and a sprinkling of finely chopped parsley.

Mix well and let the cheese melt a little before turning off the heat. Serve piping hot.

PENNE
ALL'ARRABBIATA

◆

400 g penne, 500 g ripe and firm tomatoes, 2 cloves garlic, grated pecorino, extra-virgin olive oil, salt, 1 hot red pepper.

Blanch the tomatoes in hot water, peel, remove the seeds and chop. Sauté the garlic clove in several tablespoons of oil. Add the tomatoes and let the sauce thicken over moderate heat, season with salt and the crumbled hot red pepper. Cook for a further 20 minutes over moderate heat.
Cook the pasta in plenty of boiling, salted water and drain when al dente. Mix into the sauce, turn up the heat for a few seconds, and sprinkle with grated pecorino. Remove from the heat and serve.

REGINETTE
ALLA PARMIGIANA

◆

400 g reginette, 150 g fresh grated Parmesan cheese, 100 g butter, a few sage leaves, 1 clove garlic, nutmeg, salt and pepper.

Prepare the sauce while the pasta is cooking in salted water.
Over low heat, melt the butter, add the sage leaves and the crushed garlic clove. As soon as the butter has melted and is beginning to colour (do not let it turn dark brown), remove from the heat and

discard the aromatic herbs. Dilute the melted butter with a few tablespoons of cooking water from the pasta, and add the grated Parmesan, mixing well to blend. Flavour with a little salt and grated nutmeg.
Drain the reginette when al dente and transfer to the pan with the Parmesan sauce. Turn up the heat.
Stir well to blend all the ingredients, add a little freshly ground pepper, remove from the heat, and serve.

SPAGHETTI
WITH VEGETARIAN
CARBONARA

400 g spaghetti, 6 zucchini, 1 onion, 1/2 pepper, 1 cabbage leaf, 2 eggs, nutmeg, grated Parmesan cheese, extra-virgin olive oil, salt.

Wash and slice the vegetables. Sauté the sliced onion in oil, add the chopped pepper, the cabbage leaf and zucchini. Season with salt, cover the pan, and cook for a little over 15 minutes.
In the meantime, boil the pasta. Beat the eggs mixed with a little salt and grated nutmeg. When the pasta is al dente, drain and transfer to the pan with the vegetables, add the oil and the beaten egg. Stir over moderate heat for about 2 minutes to blend the flavours.
Serve with the grated Parmesan on the side.

SPAGHETTI WITH GARLIC, OIL AND HOT RED PEPPER

◆

400 g spaghetti, 4 cloves garlic, 1 glass extra-virgin olive oil, salt, 1 hot red pepper.

Considered something of a 'classic', this recipe, one of the quickest and easiest to prepare, is certain to be a success.

Boil the pasta in plenty of salted water. In the meantime, sauté in a pan the crushed hot red pepper and the finely chopped garlic in a few tablespoons of oil.

For a sauce that is less spicy, remove the hot red pepper from the oil before adding the garlic. For a more delicate garlic taste, let the garlic flavour the oil but remove it before heating the oil with the hot red pepper.

SPAGHETTI WITH BRANDY

◆

400 g spaghetti, 4 small glasses brandy, 70 g grated Parmesan cheese, 100 g butter, 1 stock cube.

While this recipe seems most unusual, it is really quick to prepare and very tasty. Cook the pasta in plenty of salted water while you are preparing the sauce. In a non-stick saucepan, over moderate heat, melt the stock cube in the brandy. Stir constantly with a wooden spoon to keep the brandy from evaporating entirely. Add the butter, which has been left to soften at room temperature and cut into pieces, and then the Parmesan cheese.

Drain the spaghetti when al dente and mix into the sauce. You can sprinkle with more Parmesan before serving.

SPAGHETTI WITH TOMATO SAUCE

📷

400 g spaghetti, 800 g ripe and firm tomatoes, a few basil leaves, 1 teaspoon sugar, extra-virgin olive oil, salt, ground hot red pepper.

This is probably the most classic of traditional sauces with a tomato base: 'pommarola', considered the sauce par excellence for accompanying pasta.

Wash the tomatoes, blanch them in boiling water, peel them, remove the seeds and stalks, and pass them through a food mill. If there is too much water, leave the tomatoes on a sloping surface for about 15 minutes to let the excess liquid drain off, then cook over moderate heat with a little oil.

Simmer until the mixture thickens (about 30 minutes), seasoning with a pinch of salt and a teaspoon of sugar (to reduce the acid taste of the tomatoes).

72

Just before turning off the heat, add the hot red pepper and crushed basil. Boil the spaghetti and drain when al dente. Then serve in individual portions, each with a generous amount of sauce and a drizzle of olive oil.

SPAGHETTI ALLA NORMA

📷

400 g spaghetti, 600 g tomato pulp, 100 g grated mature ricotta, 3 aubergines, 1 onion, a few basil leaves, extra-virgin olive oil, salt, ground hot red pepper.

Clean the aubergines and cut into slices about 1 cm thick; sprinkle with salt, and leave for two hours on paper towels to eliminate the bitter juices. Rinse, dry well, cut into cubes and fry in oil. Leave to dry on paper towels.
Chop the onion and sauté it in several tablespoons of oil. Add the tomatoes, season with salt and hot red pepper, and let thicken over moderate heat.
Boil the pasta, drain when al dente, and transfer to a serving bowl. Mix with the tomato sauce, the fried aubergine, the grated mature ricotta and the crushed basil leaves. Mix thoroughly and serve.

SPAGHETTI WITH AUBERGINES

◆

400 g spaghetti, 3 long aubergines, 2 cloves garlic, 1 small bunch parsley, extra-virgin olive oil, salt.

Wash and dry the aubergines. Cut into quite thick slices, place on a sloping surface (a plate will do), and sprinkle with coarse salt to eliminate the bitter juices. After about 2 hours, rinse the slices, drain well, dry, and fry in plenty of oil with a little crushed garlic. When done, lay the slices on paper towels to drain off excess oil.
Boil the spaghetti and when al dente, drain, mix with the aubergines in a warmed serving dish and sprinkle with a little chopped parsley. Serve hot.

SPAGHETTI WITH CHICORY

◆

400 g spaghetti, 4 heads of chicory, 1/2 onion, 150 g Fontina cheese (optional), 1/2 glass cream, extra-virgin olive oil, nutmeg, salt and pepper.

Wash the chicory thoroughly and cut it into strips. Sauté the finely chopped onion in a few tablespoons of oil. Add the chicory, cover the pot and simmer over low heat.
Before turning off the heat, season with salt and a generous amount of freshly ground pepper. In the meantime, boil the spaghetti and drain when al dente; transfer to the pot with the chicory. Mix well with the cream and

the Fontina cheese, cut into little cubes. Sprinkle with grated nutmeg.

SPAGHETTI
WITH PUMPKIN SAUCE

◆

400 g spaghetti, 500 g yellow pumpkin (the bumpy kind is best), 500 g onions, 50 g grated Parmesan cheese, 50 g grated pecorino, 1 glass dry white wine, extra-virgin olive oil, salt and pepper.

Cut the skin off the pumpkin and dice the pulp. Finely chop the onions and sauté with the pumpkin in oil. Cover the pot and simmer over moderate heat. As soon as the pumpkin is done, uncover the pot, season with salt and pepper, and add the wine. Turn up the heat and let the wine evaporate, stirring constantly and mashing the pumpkin with a wooden spoon.

In the meantime, cook the spaghetti in plenty of boiling, salted water, drain and transfer to a serving dish. Add the pasta to the pumpkin sauce and the grated cheese. Mix well before serving.

SPAGHETTI, CHEESE
AND PEPPER

📷

400 g spaghetti, 150 g grated pecorino, salt and pepper.

Boil the spaghetti in abundant hot, salted water and drain when al dente, reserving a little cooking water.
Pour this water into a large serving bowl, add the pecorino and plenty of freshly ground pepper. Mix well, then fold in the spaghetti. Serve piping hot. In the original recipe, no oil or butter is included in the pasta sauce.

SPAGHETTI
WITH WALNUTS

◆

400 g spaghetti, 400 g walnuts, 100 g cream, 1 clove garlic, 1 handful breadcrumbs, extra-virgin olive oil, salt, nutmeg.

Moisten the breadcrumbs in a little water (or milk) and squeeze them dry. Shell the walnuts and blanch them by putting them in boiling water and peeling off the skin.
Pound the walnuts in a mortar with the garlic clove, then add the breadcrumbs and a handful of salt. Use the pestle like a spoon, mixing the ingredients together to form a smooth cream.
In a saucepan, warm the nut mixture over moderate heat, diluting with the cream and a few tablespoons of oil. Remove from the heat before the sauce boils.

Drain the spaghetti when al dente and flavour with the walnut sauce. Sprinkle with a little grated nutmeg.

SPAGHETTI WITH DRIED BROAD BEANS

◆

400 g whole-grain spaghetti, 250 g dried broad beans, 3 tomatoes, 1 onion, gomashio, extra-virgin olive oil, salt.

Soak the dried broad beans for 24 hours. Drain and remove the skins, which should come away easily. Cook them in a pot, with enough fresh water to cover them (it is important to change the water, since the beans expel toxins while soaking), the finely chopped onion, and the tomatoes, which have been washed and sliced.

Simmer in a covered pot over low heat for about 2 hours. When the beans are cooked and almost all of the water has been absorbed, add oil (two or three tablespoons) and salt.

Cook the pasta, in boiling, salted water, drain when al dente, then mix it with the beans. Mix thoroughly, sprinkle with gomashio, and serve.

SPAGHETTI WITH BEAN SAUCE

◆

400 g whole-grain spaghetti, 120 g beans (if possible, white Spanish beans), 10 chives, 1 sprig rosemary, a few bay leaves, 1 teaspoon tarragon, gomashio, extra-virgin olive oil, salt.

Soak the beans in cold water with a bay leaf for about 14 hours. Drain, rinse, and cook in fresh water with the rosemary. When the beans are done, pass through a food mill and stir to a cream, adding a little cooking water if necessary. (The same water can also be used for cooking the pasta). Flavour the bean sauce with oil, salt, and the aromatic herbs, which have been chopped and mixed together.

Boil the spaghetti in abundant salted water, drain when al dente and mix with the bean mixture in a large serving bowl. Sprinkle with gomashio and serve.

SEDANINI AND ZUCCHINI

◆

400 g sedanini, 500 g zucchini, 1 clove garlic, a bunch parsley or mint, cream (optional), extra-virgin olive oil, grated Parmesan cheese, salt and pepper.

Clean the zucchini and slice it in rounds. Slice the garlic. Heat some oil in a pan, and sauté the sliced garlic and zucchini. Stir carefully to avoid breaking the zucchini. Add salt and pepper, and sprinkle with chopped parsley or mint.

Boil the pasta in plenty of salted water, drain when al dente and transfer to the pan with the zucchini.

Mix the pasta with the sauce, adding a little cream if desired, and serve with grated Parmesan.

TAGLIATELLE WITH ASPARAGUS

◆

400 g tagliatelle (recipe on page 138), 2 bunches of asparagus, 2 teaspoons lemon juice, 2.5 dl milk, nutmeg, extra-virgin olive oil, salt and pepper.

Clean the asparagus, slice the tips and the soft part of the stalks, and sauté in a few tablespoons of oil. Add salt, pepper, nutmeg and a little less than 1/2 a glass of hot water. Cover and simmer over moderate heat for 15 minutes; as soon as the water has dried up, add the lemon juice.

Cook the asparagus until tender, adding milk from time to time. Mix the sauce in a blender, heat again, and stir in with the cooked tagliatelle.

Wild asparagus can also be used for this dish. Gather it only in unpolluted areas, and use only the tenderest parts.

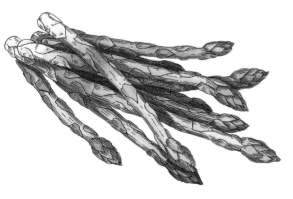

TAGLIATELLE WITH HERBS

◆

400 g tagliatelle (recipe on page 138), 1 bunch of herbs (including savory, marjoram, basil, parsley, chives and thyme), extra-virgin olive oil, salt.

Prepare the equivalent of 2 teaspoons of finely chopped herbs for each person (more savory can be used, while the thyme and chives should be used sparingly). In the meantime, boil the pasta, draining it while still al dente. Sprinkle with the herb mixture, pour over plenty of olive oil, and serve.

Obviously, fresh herbs give better results, but in the absence of these, dried herbs can be used. Chop them finely and steep them in oil for about fifteen minutes before using.

TAGLIATELLE WITH PEAS

◆

400 g tagliatelle (recipe on page 138), 500 g fresh hulled peas, 400 g ripe and firm tomatoes, 1 onion, 1 carrot, 1 bunch parsley, extra-virgin olive oil, salt and pepper.

Chop the onion and carrot, and sauté them in a saucepan with a little oil. Stir in the peas and let the flavours blend.

Blanch the tomatoes in boiling water, peel, seed and chop them, then add to the sauce. Season with salt and pepper and simmer, adding a little hot water from time to time.

Just before you turn off the heat, add the chopped parsley. Boil the tagliatelle in plenty of salted water, drain while still al dente, and stir in half the sauce. Serve with the rest of the sauce spooned over the pasta.

This sauce can also be made without tomatoes, using two onions rather than one. In another variation, a little cream is added to the sauce at the end of cooking.

TAGLIATELLE
WITH TALEGGIO CHEESE
AND TRUFFLES

400 g tagliatelle (recipe on page 138), 150 g Taleggio cheese, 1 small black truffle, 1/2 glass cream, dry white wine, butter, grated Parmesan cheese, salt and pepper.

Scrape the rind off the Taleggio without removing it completely; cut the cheese into small pieces. Warm it gently in a saucepan with a tablespoon of butter and the cream, stirring until the sauce is smooth and creamy. Season with salt and pepper.

In the meantime, boil the tagliatelle, drain while still al dente, and pour them into the saucepan with the cheese sauce, mixing well. Brush the truffle and rinse it in a little white wine; grate it over the pasta before serving it with grated Parmesan cheese.

TRENETTE
WITH WHITE CABBAGE

◆

400 g trenette, 500 g white cabbage, 2 carrots, 1 onion, 2 bay leaves, dry white wine, extra-virgin olive oil, salt.

Wash the onion, chop it finely, sauté it rapidly in a little oil with the bay leaves over high heat for a few minutes. Add the cleaned and sliced carrots, stirring occasionally.

In the meantime, clean the white cabbage, shred it very fine, and add it to the pan. Cover and simmer with the other vegetables for about twenty minutes over moderate heat. When the cabbage is wilted and the sauce almost done, pour in the white wine, let it evaporate, salt to taste, and continue cooking until done.

Boil the trenette, drain while still al dente, and pour them into the pan with the vegetables. Keep on the heat for a few more minutes, stirring continuously, then serve piping hot in a soup tureen.

TAGLIOLINI
WITH MASCARPONE

◆

400 g tagliolini (recipe on page 138), 150 g mascarpone cheese, 3 egg yolks, 4-5 tablespoons of grated Parmesan cheese, grated nutmeg, salt and pepper.

This sauce should be prepared just a few minutes before cooking the pasta. Have the eggs at room temperature. In a saucepan, mix the yolks with the grated Parmesan, a pinch of salt and a grind of fresh pepper, stirring to form a smooth cream.

Place the saucepan over very low heat, or better still, in a double-boiler (or bain-marie). Stirring carefully, add the mascarpone and season with the grated nutmeg. Boil the pasta, drain it while still al dente, pour it into the sauce, and mix well.

To give this dish a touch of refinement, garnish it at the moment of serving with a little lumpfish roe (or real caviar) and a sprinkle of grated lemon peel.

TAGLIOLINI
IN SWEET WINE SAUCE

◆

400 g tagliolini (recipe on page 138), 2 glasses sweet white wine, 150 g speck in a single slice (smoked cured ham), 150 g cooked ham in a single slice, 300 g tomato purée, 2 glasses cream, extra-virgin olive oil, grated Parmesan cheese, salt and pepper.

Cut the speck and the cooked ham into thin strips and sauté them in a little oil until they just begin to brown. Pour in the sweet white wine and let it evaporate over low heat.

Add the tomato purée, and as soon as it begins to boil, add the cream. Season with salt and pepper, and simmer for about 10 minutes.

Boil the tagliolini in plenty of salted water, drain them while still al dente, pour them into the sauce, and mix thoroughly. Complete with a sprinkle of grated Parmesan cheese.

TRENETTE
WITH PESTO

[camera icon]

400 g trenette, about 30 basil leaves, 1 clove garlic, 2-4 teaspoons pine-nuts, 2 teaspoons grated pecorino cheese, 2 teaspoons grated Parmesan cheese, extra-virgin olive oil, salt.

Wash and dry the basil leaves, then grind them in a stone mortar with the garlic and pine-nuts (pressing the basil against the sides with circular movements rather than pounding it).

Continue grinding the ingredients, then add the grated cheeses and a pinch of salt. As soon as you have a smooth paste, add olive oil drop by drop, stirring with the pestle like a spoon to form a thick, creamy sauce. If you prefer, pesto can also be made successfully in a blender.

Boil the trenette in plenty of salted water, drain them when still al dente, and dress with the pesto sauce diluted with one tablespoon of the cooking water. Mix well and serve.

VERMICELLI WITH LEEKS

◆

400 g vermicelli, 4 medium-size leeks, 1 tomato, 2 teaspoons tamari sauce, extra-virgin olive oil, salt.

Clean the leeks carefully, removing the tougher green parts, and cut into slices of about 1 cm. Sauté the slices briefly in a saucepan in a little oil, then cover and simmer over low heat for about ten minutes. Wash and coarsely chop the tomato; add it to the leeks along with a glass of hot water, the tamari sauce and a pinch of salt. Continue to simmer for 20 minutes. Boil the pasta, draining it while still al dente, then pour over it the piping hot sauce. Mix and serve immediately.

VERMICELLI
IN RAW VEGETABLE SAUCE

◆

400 g vermicelli, 500 g small ripe and firm toma-toes, 1 carrot, 1 small onion, 1 clove garlic, basil, extra-virgin olive oil, salt, ground hot red pepper.

Blanch the tomatoes in boiling water, then peel, seed and chop them. If they are very watery, slice the tomatoes in half and leave them on a sloping surface for about 15 minutes to let the water drain off before chopping them. Slice the carrot, cut the onion into thin rings, slice the garlic, and put them all in a large bowl together with the tomatoes. Season with a generous dash of oil, a pinch of salt, a pinch of hot red pepper, the chopped basil,

and mix well. Leave the sauce in a cool place for a couple of hours.
Cook the pasta in plenty of boiling salted water, drain it while still al dente, then serve with the prepared sauce.
This basic recipe can be varied and enriched according to the seasonal availability of fresh vegetables and the creativity of each individual cook.

ZITE WITH ONION
AND BREADCRUMBS

◆

400 g zite, 2 large onions, 2 cloves garlic, 2 1/2 ta-blespoons breadcrumbs, 2 glasses white wine, oregano, 1 glass extra-virgin olive oil, salt, hot red pepper.

Slice the onions and garlic finely, and sauté in a large saucepan with the oil for a few minutes. Add the breadcrumbs, frying them lightly, but without letting the onion brown. As soon as the sauce begins to reduce, pour in the wine and season with a pinch of oregano, salt, and a little hot red pepper. In the meantime boil the zite, drain them while still al dente, and pour them into the pan with the onions and the wine, which has not yet completely evaporated. Stir thoroughly over the heat for a few more minutes, adding a little oil if necessary.

Baked *pasta*

BAKED CANNELLONI

◆

For the pasta: (recipe on page 137).
For the béchamel: (recipe on page 141).

These are three of the most classic versions of baked cannelloni: with spinach and ricotta, with ground meat and tomato, and with tuna. They can all be varied according to the taste of the cook.
All recipes start by preparing the pasta base for the cannelloni, and continue with the béchamel, according to the basic recipes. The different fillings can then be made as follows.

WITH SPINACH
AND RICOTTA FILLING

📷

500 g spinach, 250 g ricotta cheese, 2 eggs, béchamel (see page 141), grated Parmesan cheese, butter, grated nutmeg, salt and pepper.

Wash, trim, and boil the spinach in a little salted water; drain and let cool. Squeeze well, and chop finely. Mash the ricotta thoroughly in a bowl, and mix it with the spinach, egg yolks, and a few tablespoons of grated Parmesan. Season with salt, pepper and grated nutmeg. If the mixture is too stiff, add the egg whites or a drop of warm milk, then use the filling to stuff the pasta squares. Roll up the squares, and place them in an oven dish with a layer of béchamel on the bottom. Pour the rest of the béchamel over, sprinkle with grated Parmesan and dot with butter. Brown in a preheated oven at 180 °C for about half an hour.

WITH GROUND BEEF
AND TOMATO FILLING

◆

300 g ground beef, 100 g tomato pulp, 1 onion, basil, 1/2 glass red wine, béchamel (see page 141, half-quantity), 2 eggs, 100 g grated Parmesan cheese, butter, extra-virgin olive oil, salt and pepper.

In a saucepan, soften the chopped onion in a little oil, then add the ground beef, stirring so that it browns evenly. Pour in the wine, let it evaporate, season with salt and pepper, and add the tomato pulp. Cook for about 30 minutes, and add basil before removing from the heat. Let it cool, then blend in the eggs and the Parmesan. Stuff the cannelloni with this filling, then put them in an oven dish with a thin layer of béchamel on the bottom. Pour the rest of the sauce over the cannelloni, sprinkle with grated Parmesan and chopped basil, and dot with a bit of butter. Brown in a preheated oven at 180 °C for about half an hour.

WITH TUNA FILLING

◆

500 g tuna in oil, 500 g peeled tomatoes, 1 onion, 2 1/2 tablespoons capers, 1 large mozzarella, 1 bunch parsley, basil, extra-virgin olive oil, butter, salt and pepper.

Chop the tuna, mozzarella and capers very finely; season with chopped parsley and basil, and a pinch of salt and pepper. In a saucepan, sauté the chopped onion in a few spoonfuls of oil, then add the peeled and seeded tomatoes. Season with salt, and simmer over a low heat for

about 30 minutes. Add chopped parsley and pepper before removing from the heat. Stuff the cannelloni with the filling and arrange them in a buttered oven dish. Pour the tomato sauce over them and dot with bits of butter. Bake in a preheated oven (200 °C) for about 10 minutes.

CANNELLONI WITH SALMON

◆

For the pasta: (recipe on page 137).
For the sauce: 1 cup béchamel (see page 141), butter.
For the filling: 400 g salmon meat, 2 zucchini, 12 asparagus stems, 1 egg, 100 g ricotta cheese, salt.

Scald the diced zucchini and the asparagus tips in boiling salted water, then drain them well. In the blender, blend the raw salmon meat, zucchini, asparagus tips, egg and a pinch of salt. Pour the mixture into a bowl, stir in the ricotta and mix thoroughly. Cook the pasta, drain, and lay to dry on a teacloth. Place the squares on a floured surface, spread them with the filling and roll them up. Arrange the cannelloni in a buttered oven dish, pour the béchamel over them and dot with butter. Brown in a preheated oven (180 °C) for about 15 minute before serving.

CANNELLONI
WITH SPINACH AND HAM

◆

For the pasta: (recipe on page 137).
For the sauce: 1 ladleful béchamel (see page 141), butter, grated Parmesan cheese.

For the filling: 300 g spinach, 200 g thickly sliced cooked ham, 2 eggs, 150 g Fontina cheese, 50 g butter, grated Parmesan cheese, nutmeg, salt.

Wash and trim the spinach, scald in a little salted boiling water, squeeze, then finely chop. Dice the ham, melt the Fontina cheese gently in a saucepan with the butter. In a bowl, mix with a wooden spoon the spinach, ham, Fontina, a handful of grated Parmesan, the eggs, a pinch of nutmeg and one of salt. Cook the pasta, drain, and lay to dry on a teacloth. Place the pasta squares on a floured surface, spread them with the filling and roll them up. Arrange the cannelloni in a buttered ovenproof dish, pour the béchamel over them, sprinkle with grated Parmesan and dot with a few small cubes of butter. Brown in a preheated oven (180 °C) for about 15 minutes before serving.

BAKED LASAGNE

For the pasta: (recipe on page 138), 2 mozzarellas, grated Parmesan cheese, béchamel (see page 141), butter, salt.
For the sauce: 150 g ground beef, 50 g cooked ham in a single slice, 50 g sausage, 600 g tomato pulp, 1/2 onion, 1 small carrot, 1/2 celery stalk, 1 clove garlic, bay leaf, basil, 1 clove, 1 cinnamon stick, 1/2 glass red wine, extra-virgin olive oil, salt and pepper.

Prepare the pasta according to the instructions, boil it and lay to dry on a teacloth. Then prepare the sauce. Clean and chop the onion, carrot, celery, garlic,

88

and the ham. Break up the sausage with a fork and sauté it lightly in a saucepan with a little oil. Add the chopped vegetables and ham, mix well, and let them wilt. Before the sauce begins to colour, add the ground beef and brown evenly, stirring constantly. Pour in the wine, let it evaporate, then add the tomato, bay leaf, spices and salt. Lower the heat, cover, and simmer slowly for about 1 hour. The sauce should be fairly liquid, since it is to be poured over the layers of pasta. While the meat sauce is cooking, prepare the béchamel.

Put a little meat sauce and a little béchamel in the bottom of a rectangular oven dish; blend them with a wooden spoon. Spread over this a first layer of lasagne, and sprinkle over it diced mozzarella and grated Parmesan. Cover with another layer of lasagne, then spread with meat sauce and béchamel. Continue alternating the layers in this manner, until all the ingredients are used up, finishing with a layer of meat sauce and béchamel. Sprinkle with Parmesan, dot with bits of butter, and bake in a preheated oven (200 °C) for 30-40 minutes.

CANNELLONI WITH SAUSAGE AND MOZZARELLA

◆

For the pasta: (recipe on page 137).
For the sauce: 1 ladle béchamel (see page 141), 2 1/2 tablespoons tomato purée, butter, grated Parmesan cheese.
For the filling: 300 g spinach beet, 200 g sausage, 200 g mozzarella, 2 eggs, butter, grated Parmesan cheese, salt and pepper.

Wash and trim the spinach beet, scald in a little salted boiling water, squeeze, then chop finely. Skin the sausage and break up the meat with a fork, then put it in a saucepan and sauté it with the spinach beet in the butter. Cool, and pour into a bowl with the diced mozzarella, the eggs, a generous handful of grated Parmesan, a pinch of salt and one of pepper. Blend all the ingredients well together with a wooden spoon. Cook the pasta, drain, and lay to dry on a teacloth.

Place the pasta squares on a floured work board, spread them with the filling, and roll them up. Arrange the cannelloni in a buttered ovenproof dish, cover with béchamel, then spoon the tomato purée over them. Sprinkle with grated Parmesan and dot with bits of butter. Brown in a preheated oven (180 °C) for about 15 minutes before serving.

FANCY LASAGNE

◆

For the pasta: to the basic recipe on page 138 add 300 g spinach, 20 g dried powdered tomatoes, 1 pinch dried hot red pepper.
For the sauce: 200 g Gorgonzola, 150 g pork sausage, 1 leek, 1 sprig rosemary, 40 g butter, 1 cup tomato purée, 1 cup béchamel, grated Parmesan cheese, extra-virgin olive oil, salt.

Divide the pasta dough into three parts. Proceed with the first in the normal manner. To the second add the spinach - boiled in a little salted water, squeezed, and processed in the blender. Blend the dried tomato powder and a pinch of ground hot red pepper well into the

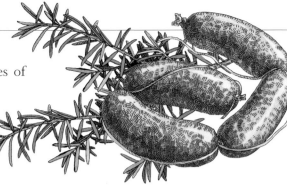

third part. Roll out the three types of pasta and cut into squares.

Chop the leek and the rosemary leaves, peel the sausage and break it up with a fork, and sauté all together in a saucepan with a little oil. Add the tomato purée and simmer for a while to reduce the water content. In another saucepan, melt the butter and Gorgonzola over very low heat. Cook the lasagne in plenty of salted water, drain, and spread a layer in a buttered ovenproof dish. Cover with a little of the meat and tomato sauce, a layer of béchamel, and one of melted Gorgonzola. Proceed with another layer of lasagne, alternating the colours, and garnish with the sauces in the same way. Continue until all the ingredients are used up, sprinkle the top layer generously with grated Parmesan and dot with a few flakes of butter. Brown in a preheated oven (180 °C) for about half an hour before serving.

LASAGNE, PIEDMONT STYLE

◆

For the pasta: (recipe on page 138).
For the sauce: 100 g ground veal, 50 g sausage, 50 g chicken livers, 1 slice cooked salami, 1 small onion, 1 celery stalk, 1 sprig rosemary, 2 bay leaves, 1 cup tomato sauce, 1 cup béchamel, grated Parmesan cheese, aged Toma d'Alba cheese, butter, extra-virgin olive oil, grated nutmeg, salt and pepper.

Chop together the onion, celery, salami and rosemary leaves; sauté them in a saucepan with the oil. Wash the chicken livers and chop them into pieces. Peel the sausage and mash the meat with a fork. Add both meats, along with the ground veal and the bay leaves, to the sautéed mixture, seasoning with salt and pepper. Cook over medium heat, mixing well with a wooden spoon. Lastly, add the tomato sauce, and leave the sauce to simmer slowly until done. Cook the lasagne and spread a first layer in a buttered ovenproof dish. Cover with a little of the sauce and some béchamel, sprinkle over a layer of grated Parmesan and one of grated Toma d'Alba cheese, and season with a little grated nutmeg. Continue building up the layers with the rest of the ingredients. Dot the top with a few flakes of butter and brown in a preheated oven (200 °C) for 30-40 minutes. Serve piping hot.

LASAGNE WITH HERBS

◆

For the pasta: (recipe on page 138).
For the sauce: 200 g spinach, 200 g spinach beet, 100 g butter, 1 clove garlic, 1 cup béchamel (see page 141), 1 sprig rosemary, grated Parmesan cheese, salt and pepper.

Wash and trim the vegetables. Cook them in a little boiling water, let cool, squeeze thoroughly and chop finely. In

91

a saucepan, melt the butter, seasoning it with the garlic and rosemary. Boil the lasagne and spread a first layer in a buttered ovenproof dish. Cover with a layer of béchamel, then one of vegetables. Sprinkle generously with grated Parmesan, moisten with the seasoned melted butter and flavour with a twist of freshly-ground pepper. Continue to add layers, finishing with one of béchamel, grated Parmesan and butter.

Brown in a preheated oven (200 °C) for 30-40 minutes and serve piping hot.

LASAGNE WITH RICOTTA AND AUBERGINES

◆

For the pasta: (recipe on page 138).
For the sauce: 300 g tomato pulp, 2 medium-sized aubergines, 180 g fresh ricotta cheese, 10 shelled walnuts, grated Parmesan cheese, extra-virgin olive oil, salt and pepper.

Prepare the basic pasta according to the instructions, then let it dry on a floured surface.

Set a saucepan on the heat and pour in a little oil and the sieved tomato pulp, season with salt and a pinch of pepper to prepare a sauce. In the meantime, blanch the walnuts, then peel and crush them. Clean, wash and dry the aubergines, slice them, sprinkle with salt, and leave to rest for a couple of hours. Pour off the water, rinse and dry the aubergine slices, then deep-fry them in boiling oil. Place the slices on paper

towels to absorb the excess oil, then chop. Bring to the boil a large pot of water. When it boils, add salt and drop in the lasagne. Boil them a few at a time, and remove while still al dente with a slotted spoon. Lay them on a teacloth to dry. Spread a first layer of lasagne in an oiled ovenproof dish and cover it with the tomato sauce. Sprinkle over it some chopped aubergines, a little crumbled ricotta, some of the crushed walnuts and grated Parmesan, moistened with a little oil.

Continue to add layers, ending with one of lasagne covered with thinly sliced ricotta, a sprinkling of Parmesan and a trickle of oil. Cook in a preheated oven (180 °C) for about ten minutes before serving.

GREEN LASAGNE
📷

For the pasta: to the basic recipe on page 138 add 300 g spinach.
For the sauce: 150 g Castelmagro cheese, 150 g Dolcelatte cheese, 150 g fresh ricotta cheese, 40 g butter, grated Parmesan cheese, salt, grated nutmeg, pepper.

For the pasta, follow the instructions in the basic recipe. Boil the spinach, drain, squeeze and process in the blender, then mix with the pasta dough.

Over very low heat, melt the butter, Dolcelatte and Castelmagro in a saucepan. Boil the pasta, and spread a first layer in a buttered ovenproof dish. Cover with a layer of the melted cheese sauce and then with one of ricotta, seasoning with a pinch of nutmeg and a grind of pepper. Continue layering the pasta and cheeses until all the ingredients are used up. Dot the top layer with a few flakes of butter, and sprinkle generously with grated Parmesan. Brown in a preheated oven (200 °C) for 30-40 minutes, then serve.

MACCHERONI PASTICCIATI

◆

400 g maccheroni, 100 g Emmental, 100 g grated Parmesan cheese, 200 g fresh mushrooms, 1 clove garlic, 1 bunch parsley, béchamel (see page 141), extra-virgin olive oil, butter, salt and pepper.

Trim the mushrooms, removing the earthy residue with a damp cloth; slice them and stew lightly in a little oil flavoured with the crushed garlic. When they are done, remove the garlic and season with salt, pepper and chopped parsley. Prepare the béchamel following the instructions, then stir in the diced Emmental and 1 ½ tablespoons of stewed mushrooms. Boil the pasta in plenty of salted

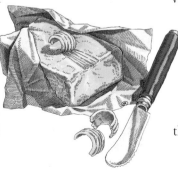

water, drain it while still al dente, and mix in the mushrooms. In a buttered ovenproof dish, arrange alternate layers of the pasta and mushroom mixture, and the béchamel and grated Parmesan. Finish with a layer of béchamel and Parmesan, and dot with a few flakes of butter. Bake in a preheated oven (180 °C) for 15 minutes.

BAKED PIZZOCCHERI

📷

300 g pizzoccheri (type of tagliatelle), 150 g grated Parmesan cheese, 150 g soft cheese (Fontina or Bitto), 200 g white cabbage or spinach beet, 200 g potatoes, 3 cloves garlic, 1 sprig sage, 100 g butter, extra-virgin olive oil, salt.

Wash the cabbage and potatoes, cut them in pieces and boil both in plenty of salted water. Put the pizzoccheri to boil in the same water, calculating the cooking times so that all the ingredients can be drained al dente at the same time. Meanwhile, cut the soft cheese into thin slices and melt the butter with a few spoonfuls of oil, flavouring with the sage and the crushed garlic cloves (removing the latter as soon as they begin to colour).

Spread a first layer of pasta and vegetables in an ovenproof dish. Sprinkle with grated Parmesan and the slices of soft cheese, and season with the sage-flavoured butter. Continue building up these layers, then complete

with a generous sprinkling of Parmesan and dot with a few flakes of butter. Crisp in a preheated oven (200 °C) for about 10 minutes.

MACCHERONI AND AUBERGINE PASTICCIO

◆

400 g maccheroni, 4 aubergines, 800 g tomato pulp, 1 onion, a few basil leaves, 2 mozzarellas or 150 g Caciocavallo cheese, grated Parmesan cheese, extra-virgin olive oil, sugar, salt, hot red pepper.

Clean and slice the aubergines, sprinkle them with salt, and let drain for half an hour. Then rinse and dry them well and cook on a cast-iron griddle.

Prepare the sauce by sautéing the thinly sliced onion in a few spoonfuls of oil, then adding the tomato. Stir in a pinch of sugar, salt and hot red pepper. Simmer over moderate heat for about 20 minutes, adding the basil just before removing the pan from the heat.

In the meantime, boil the pasta in plenty of salted water, drain it while still quite al dente, and dress with a trickle of oil. In a buttered ovenproof dish, start with a layer of tomato sauce, followed by one of sliced aubergines, one of sliced mozzarella, and one of pasta, completing with a sprinkling of Parmesan. Continue layering in this order until all the ingredients are used up. Finish with a layer of tomato sauce, sprinkled with Parmesan and a few basil leaves. Cook in a preheated oven (180 °C) for about 20 minutes before serving.

A richer version of this traditional Sicilian dish uses lard in the tomato sauce, while the aubergines are dusted lightly with flour and fried in boiling oil.

FISH PASTICCIO

◆

For the pasta: (recipe on page 138).
For the sauce: 250 g squid, 200 g clams, 200 g mussels, 100 g scampi, 500 g peeled tomatoes, 3 cloves garlic, 1 bunch parsley, béchamel (see page 141), 1 glass dry white wine, extra-virgin olive oil, salt, 1 hot red pepper.

Prepare the pasta, boil in plenty of salted water and let dry on a tea cloth. Then prepare the sauce. Clean the different types of fish. Cut the squid in strips. Put the shellfish to open in a covered frying-pan over high heat – as they open, remove the molluscs from the shells and when you have finished, strain the cooking liquid and set aside. In a saucepan, gently heat a few spoonfuls of oil, flavouring it with 2 cloves of garlic. As soon as it begins to colour, remove the garlic and add the squid; five minutes later, add the rest of the fish. Pour in the wine and, as soon as it has evaporated, the shellfish cooking liquid. Then add the chopped, peeled tomatoes, and the crumbled hot red pepper. Continue simmering for 15-20 minutes. Finely chop the parsley and the remaining clove of garlic, add to the sauce and salt to taste, then cook for another few minutes before turning off the heat. Now prepare the béchamel.

Spread a layer of fish sauce and béchamel in the bottom of an ovenproof dish and cover with a layer of pasta. Continue layering in this way until all the ingredients are used up. Finish with a layer of fish sauce and sprinkle the surface with basil leaves. Brown in a preheated oven (200 °C) for about half an hour before serving.

a few tablespoons of mushrooms. Boil the pasta in abundant salted water, drain it while al dente, and mix it with the sautéed mushrooms and sausage. In an ovenproof dish, form alternating layers of pasta, béchamel and grated Parmesan. Complete with a layer of béchamel, topped with grated Parmesan and dotted with butter. Bake in a moderate oven, around 200 °C, for about 15 minutes. After removing the dish from the oven, let it rest a few minutes before serving.

RIGATONI PASTICCIATI

◆

380 g rigatoni, 200 g mushrooms, 150 g sausage, 1 clove garlic, 100 g grated Parmesan cheese, butter, béchamel (see page 141), extra-virgin olive oil, salt and pepper.

Trim and wash the mushrooms, slice and sauté gently in a little olive oil with the skinned and sliced sausage, and a crushed clove of garlic. When the mushrooms are done, discard the garlic; season with salt and pepper. Prepare a rather liquid béchamel sauce, then add

BAKED TAGLIATELLE WITH ASPARAGUS

◆

400 g tagliatelle (recipe on page 138), 1 kg asparagus, 250 g fresh ricotta cheese, 2 eggs, grated nutmeg, grated Parmesan cheese, extra-virgin olive oil, salt and pepper.

Clean the asparagus, cutting off the tougher parts of the stalks, and cook in boiling salted water for about 15 minutes. Drain and leave to drip, then chop into pieces, discarding any parts that are still tough. Heat a little oil in a wide saucepan and sauté the asparagus until golden. Meanwhile, place the ricotta in a bowl and blend it with a little water, salt, and pepper to form a smooth cream. Heat a large pot of water for the pasta, bring it to the boil, salt it and drop in the tagliatelle, draining them while still al dente. Stir olive oil and grated Parmesan into the pasta, then spread a first layer in an oiled ovenproof dish.

Cover this with half the asparagus and half the ricotta cream. Then proceed with another layer of tagliatelle, one of asparagus and ricotta, and finishing with a layer of pasta.

Beat the eggs, season with a little salt, pepper, and a pinch of grated nutmeg, and stir in 1 1/2 tablespoons of grated Parmesan. Pour this over the top of the pasta, and brown in a preheated oven (180 °C) for about half an hour.

CAULIFLOWER TIMBALLO

◆

400 g lasagne (recipe on page 138), 1 large cauliflower, 1 clove garlic, 1 pinch grated nutmeg, ground hot red pepper, béchamel (see page 141), 100 g grated Gruyère, 100 g grated Parmesan cheese, extra-virgin olive oil, salt.

Prepare the lasagne according to the instructions, boil in plenty of salted water, drain and let dry on a teacloth. Wash the cauliflower, cut it into florets, boil for a few minutes in a little water, and drain. Sauté the cauliflower in a little oil in a frying-pan with the garlic, a pinch of hot red pepper and one of grat-

ed nutmeg. Then prepare the béchamel, following the instructions given and adding a handful of grated Parmesan and one of Gruyère.

In an oiled ovenproof dish, start with a layer of lasagne, followed by the béchamel, the grated Parmesan and Gruyère, and lastly the cauliflower. Repeat the process until all the ingredients are used up, finishing with a layer of béchamel and the grated cheeses. Bake in a preheated oven (200 °C) until a golden crust has formed on the top (about 15 minutes).

FENNEL TIMBALLO

◆

400 g lasagne (recipe on page 138), 1 kg fennel, 1 clove garlic, 1 pinch grated nutmeg, béchamel (see page 141), 100 g grated Gruyère, 100 g grated Parmesan cheese, extra-virgin olive oil, salt, ground hot red pepper.

Prepare the lasagne according to the instructions, boil in plenty of salted water, drain, and let dry on a teacloth. Wash

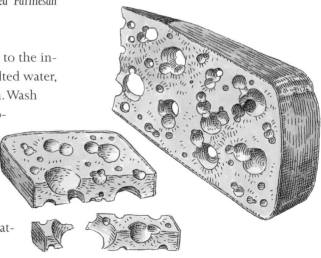

the fennel carefully, cut the heads vertically into wedges and blanch in a little salted water. Drain the wedges while still al dente, then sauté in a little oil in a frying-pan with the garlic, a pinch of hot red pepper, and one of grated nutmeg. Then prepare the béchamel, following the instructions given, adding a handful of grated Parmesan and one of Gruyère.

In an oiled ovenproof dish, start with a layer of lasagne, followed by the béchamel, the grated Parmesan and Gruyère, and lastly the fennel. Repeat the process until all the ingredients are used up, finishing with a layer of béchamel and the grated cheeses. Bake in a preheated oven (200 °C) until the top is crispy and golden.

PEPPER TIMBALLO

◆

400 g lasagne (recipe on page 138), 3 peppers, 2 ripe plum tomatoes, 1 onion, 1 large mozzarella, tomato sauce as required, grated Parmesan cheese, extra-virgin olive oil, salt, ground hot red pepper.

Prepare the lasagne according to the instructions, boil in plenty of salted water, drain, and let dry on a teacloth. If you do not have any ready-made, prepare a good tomato sauce, starting with a sauté of finely-chopped carrot, celery and onion, and adding a little basil when almost done. Wash the peppers, remove the seeds and the white inner parts, and cut into strips. Place the peppers and the thinly sliced onion in a large frying-pan with a little oil, and sauté over high heat for a few minutes, stirring with a wooden spoon; then lower the heat. When the peppers begin to soften, add two diced plum tomatoes, then season with salt and hot red pepper only towards the end of cooking.

As soon as the peppers are done, spread a layer of lasagne in an oiled ovenproof dish. Cover this with tomato sauce and sprinkle with diced mozzarella, grated Parmesan, and peppers.

Repeat the layers until all the ingredients are used up, ending with a layer of lasagne, tomato sauce and grated Parmesan. Bake in a preheated oven (200 °C) for about twenty minutes, then serve.

TIMBALLO CAPRICCIOSO

◆

400 g lasagne (recipe on page 138), 800 g ripe and firm tomatoes, 1 mozzarella, 2 aubergines, 2 peppers, 2 zucchini, 2 onions, 1 carrot, 1 celery stalk, oregano, grated Parmesan cheese, extra-virgin olive oil, salt, ground hot red pepper.

Prepare the lasagne as instructed, boil in plenty of salted water, drain, and let dry on a teacloth. Wash, dry, and cut into pieces the aubergines, zucchini and peppers (seeded, and with the white inner parts removed). Place all the vegetables in a frying-pan with the thinly-sliced onions and a little oil. Sauté for a few minutes over moderate heat. Then lower the heat and leave to simmer, adding a little salt and a pinch of hot red pepper just before removing from the heat.

Meanwhile, prepare a tomato sauce. Blanch the tomatoes in boiling water for a few minutes, then peel, seed and chop them. Finely chop the onion, celery and carrot, and cook with the tomatoes and a pinch of oregano. When the sauce is nearly done, pour it into the pan with the other vegetables and stir gently over the heat for a few minutes to let the flavours blend.

Spread a layer of lasagne in an oiled ovenproof dish, cover it with the tomato and vegetable sauce, then sprinkle with diced mozzarella and grated Parmesan. Repeat the layers until all the ingredients are used up, finishing with a layer of lasagne, tomato and Parmesan. Bake in a preheated oven (200 °C) for about twenty minutes.

VEGETARIAN TIMBALLO

◆

400 g spaghetti, 300 g fresh hulled peas, 3 artichokes, 1/2 onion, 100 g Gruyère, 1 lemon, breadcrumbs, extra-virgin olive oil, salt, ground hot red pepper.

Remove the tough outer leaves from the artichokes, cut off the tips, cut into thin wedges, and place in water mixed with a little lemon juice.

Slice the onion thinly and sauté it in a frying pan with a little oil for a few minutes. Add the peas and artichokes, season with salt and hot red pepper, cover, and simmer over moderate heat.

When the vegetables are almost done, bring a large pot of salted water to the boil, and add the spaghetti.

Drain while still al dente and season with a trickle of oil. In an oiled ovenproof dish, spread a layer of spaghetti

Trim the spinach, wash carefully, and cook in a little lightly salted water. Drain and squeeze well, then chop finely and mix with the mashed ricotta. Add a little of the spinach cooking water or milk, if necessary, until the mixture has a smooth, creamy consistency. Complete by stirring in the grated Parmesan, a pinch of salt, one of hot red pepper and one of grated nutmeg.

Spread a layer of lasagne in an oiled ovenproof dish, cover with a layer of spinach and ricotta, and sprinkle with grated Parmesan. Repeat the layers in the same way until all the ingredients are used up, ending with a layer of spinach and Parmesan.

Bake in a preheated moderate oven until the top is golden (about half an hour).

and cover with the thinly-sliced Gruyère. Spread the vegetables in the middle, and cover with another layer of spaghetti. Sprinkle the top with breadcrumbs and bake in a preheated oven (180 °C) for about twenty minutes. Turn out onto a serving-dish and serve hot.

SPINACH TIMBALLO
◆

400 g lasagne (recipe on page 138), 1 kg spinach, 400 g ricotta cheese, 100 g grated Parmesan cheese, 1 pinch grated nutmeg, extra-virgin olive oil, salt, ground hot red pepper.

Prepare the lasagne as instructed, boil in plenty of salted water, drain, and let dry on a teacloth.

BUCATINI PIE
◆

200 g bucatini, 400 g potatoes, 200 g peeled tomatoes, 2 onions, oregano, basil, 50 g grated Parmesan cheese, 2 tablespoons extra-virgin olive oil, salt and pepper.

Peel and slice the potatoes. Spread a layer of sliced potatoes in the bottom of a high-sided cake pan. Sieve the tomatoes, or pass them through a food-mill, and pour a little of the purée over the potatoes. Slice one of the onions very finely and scatter it over the potatoes and tomato purée. Pour over it 1 1/2 tablespoons of oil, a little grated Parmesan, salt, pepper, and a generous sprinkling of oregano and basil. Over this, spread a layer of bucatini broken into pieces. Repeat the layers of potatoes, tomatoes, onion and bucatini, seasoning as before. Finish with a layer of potatoes, since the pasta should be buried in the middle of the pie. Add enough water to cover the pasta layers and bake in a preheated moderate oven for about 30 minutes, or until the water has been absorbed.

VINCISGRASSI

◆

For the pasta: 400 g flour, 200 g semolina, 5 eggs, 40 g butter, Vin Santo (sweet wine), salt.
For the béchamel: (see page 141).
For the sauce: 100 g bacon fat, 1 onion, 300 g chicken giblets, 450 g veal sweetbreads and bone marrow, 250 g tomato pulp, grated nutmeg, white wine, stock as required, 200 g grated Parmesan cheese, butter, extra-virgin olive oil, salt and pepper.

Put the flour, semolina, eggs, melted butter, a little salt, and a finger of Vin Santo into a bowl and mix thoroughly. Knead well and let rest for about half an hour. Roll the pasta out thin; cut it into strips

about 10-15 cm long. Boil it in plenty of salted water. When it is half-cooked, drain, and let dry on teacloths.

Prepare the sauce: chop the bacon fat and onion and sauté them in oil in a saucepan. Add the finely chopped chicken giblets, brown them for a few minutes while stirring, then pour in the white wine. As soon as it has evaporated, add the tomato pulp, season with salt, pepper and a pinch of grated nutmeg, and cook for about a quarter of an hour. Add the chopped sweetbreads and bone marrow; salt, cover and simmer for about an hour and a half, adding hot stock if necessary.

In the meantime, prepare the béchamel following the instructions given.

Butter an ovenproof dish and spread layers of pasta, a little béchamel, grated Parmesan, sauce, and a few spoonfuls of butter. Repeat the layers until all the ingredients are used up, ending with a layer of past,a covered with béchamel and grated Parmesan. Cook in a preheated oven at 200 °C for 30-40 minutes. Serve piping hot.

Gnocchi
and filled pasta

AGNOLOTTI WITH BASS

For the pasta: (recipe on page 138).
For the filling: 250 g bass, 50 g ricotta cheese, 1 egg, 2 teaspoons grated Parmesan cheese, 1 sprig basil, grated nutmeg, butter, salt.
For the sauce: 8 artichoke hearts, 1 lemon, 2 sage leaves, 50 g butter.

Lightly brown the fish in a little butter, then remove the bones and skin and mash it with a fork. Beat the egg in a bowl, season with a pinch of salt and one of grated nutmeg. Add the ricotta, the fish, 2 teaspoons of grated Parmesan and the chopped basil, and blend all the ingredients thoroughly. Roll out the pasta, made according to the basic recipe, and place small mounds of the filling on it at equal distances. Cover with a second layer of pasta, then press down with your fingertips around each filled section to eliminate air bubbles. With a pastry wheel, cut into 3 cm squares.
Cut the artichoke hearts into small wedges, dip them in water mixed with a little lemon juice, drain, and sauté lightly in a little butter. Melt the rest of the butter in another saucepan, flavouring it with the sage. Cook the agnolotti in plenty of salted water, drain, and pour into a large serving bowl. Stir in the artichoke hearts, dress with the melted butter, and serve immediately.

AGNOLOTTI NEAPOLITAN STYLE

For the pasta: (recipe on page 138).
For the filling: 300 g ricotta cheese, 2 eggs, 1 large mozzarella, 1 handful basil leaves, salt and pepper.
For the sauce: 500 g tomato pulp, 1 onion, a few basil leaves, 300 g beef, red wine, extra-virgin olive oil, salt and pepper.

Start by preparing the pasta for the agnolotti according to the instructions. Then prepare the filling by blending the ricotta in a bowl with the 2 eggs, the basil, the chopped mozzarella, a pinch of salt, and a dash of freshly-ground pepper.
To prepare the sauce, wilt the chopped onion in an earthenware pot with a few spoonfuls of oil, then add the meat cut into pieces and sauté, stirring constantly. Season with salt, sprinkle a little red wine over it, cook for a few minutes and then add the tomato pulp. Simmer over low heat for about an hour. Before removing from the heat, add the pepper and the basil leaves torn into pieces.
Roll out the pasta on a floured surface and cut it into large disks. Place a little of the filling at the centre of each disk, then fold up the pasta to form the agnolotti, pressing the edges tightly together to eliminate any air bubbles.

Boil the agnolotti in plenty of salted water, drain, and serve with the meat sauce. If desired, sprinkle with Parmesan cheese.

AGNOLOTTI
WITH TRUFFLES

◆

For the pasta: (recipe on page 138).
For the filling: 150 g lean pork, 150 g Parma ham, 100 g veal, 1/2 black or white truffle, 1 egg, dry white wine (optional), grated Parmesan cheese, 50 g butter, salt and pepper.
For the sauce: 1/2 truffle, grated Parmesan cheese, butter.

Prepare the pasta for the agnolotti according to the instructions. Place in a saucepan: the butter, the ground veal and pork, the chopped ham, half the truffle (cleaned and sliced thinly using a special truffle-slicer), the egg, a handful of grated Parmesan, salt and pepper. Cook over low heat, stirring well and moistening with a little white wine only if necessary.
When the filling is thoroughly cooked, roll the pasta into a large sheet and place

small heaps of the filling at equal distances over half of it. Fold over the other half, press down, and cut into the desired shapes with a pastry wheel. Leave the agnolotti to dry on a teacloth for about half an hour.
Bring a large pot of salted water to the boil and drop in the agnolotti, removing them with a slotted spoon as soon as they come to the surface. Place them on a hot serving-dish, sprinkle with grated Parmesan and melted butter, and complete the dish by grating over them the half truffle not used in the filling.

POTATO AGNOLOTTI

◆

For the pasta: (recipe on page 138).
For the filling: 600 g potatoes, 1 onion, 3 mint leaves, 1 pinch cinnamon, 1 shot cognac, butter, salt and pepper.
For the sauce: grated smoked ricotta cheese, butter.

Prepare the pasta for the agnolotti following the instructions given.
Boil, peel and mash the potatoes, then stir in the salt and pepper, the cognac, chopped mint and a pinch of cinnamon. Mix the ingredients well. Then slice the onion finely, sauté lightly in a little butter and blend into the potato mixture.
Roll the pasta out in a large sheet. Place piles of the filling at equal distances over half of it, fold over the other half, and press down with your fingertips around each filled section. Cut out the agnolotti with a pastry wheel.

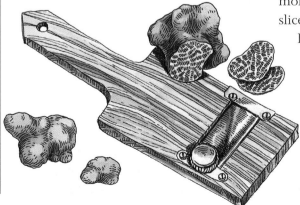

Bring a large pot of water to the boil, salt lightly and drop in the agnolotti. Drain and serve dressed with the melted butter, and sprinkled with the grated smoked ricotta.

SPINACH DUMPLINGS

◆

300 g stale bread, 800 g spinach, 1 glass milk, 2 eggs, 1 small onion, 1 clove garlic, 2 teaspoons flour, 1 1/2 tablespoons breadcrumbs, 2 tablespoons grated Parmesan cheese, 1 pinch grated nutmeg, 100 g butter, salt and pepper.

Among the many different recipes for dumplings we have chosen this one, since it is the most suitable for serving without broth.
Start by dicing the stale bread and soaking it in warm milk. Trim and wash the spinach, then boil it in a little salted water or steam it. Chop the garlic and onion and sauté in a large saucepan in a little butter. Add the drained and squeezed spinach and continue to sauté over moderate heat. In a large bowl, mix the beaten eggs with the bread, add the spinach and blend thoroughly. Season with salt, a pinch of pepper and the grated nutmeg, then stir in the flour and breadcrumbs. Shape the mixture into small dumplings, drop them into a large pot of boiling salted water and cook for 15 minutes with the water boiling gently.
Remove with a slotted spoon, serve dressed with the melted butter and sprinkled with grated Parmesan.

CASONCELLI

◆

For the pasta: 500 g white flour, 1 pinch salt, 5 eggs.
For the filling: 300 g beef, 1 carrot, 1 small celery stalk, 1/2 onion, 1 clove, 1 pinch grated nutmeg, 3-4 basil leaves, 1 egg yolk, 1/2 glass full-bodied red wine, 50 g grated Parmesan cheese, 50 g fine breadcrumbs, butter, 1 1/2 tablespoons extra-virgin olive oil, salt and pepper.
For the sauce: a few sage leaves, 100 g grated Grana cheese, 120 g butter.

On a floured board, mix the flour with a pinch of salt, four whole eggs and one yolk, adding a little water if necessary. Knead well for about ten minutes, then roll two thin sheets, being careful not to let them dry out.
In a saucepan, sauté the thinly sliced onion in a rounded tablespoon of butter and the olive oil. Add the beef and brown it on all sides, then sprinkle with the wine and let it evaporate. Clean and chop the carrot and celery. Add them to the saucepan with the meat, along with the clove, chopped basil, salt, pepper and a pinch of grated nutmeg. Simmer covered for two and a half hours, adding a little hot water from time to time if necessary.
When done, dice the meat and pass the vegetables through a food-mill. Pour the meat and vegetables into a bowl, add the breadcrumbs, the grated Grana and the egg yolk. Blend all the ingredients thoroughly, and salt to taste.
Place small heaps of this mixture at equal distances on one sheet of pasta. Lay the second sheet over the first and

press down with your fingertips around each filled section to seal thoroughly. Use a pastry wheel to cut it into squares about 4 cm. Let them dry on a lightly floured teacloth.

Cook the casoncelli in plenty of boiling salted water for about 10 minutes, drain thoroughly, and pour into a hot serving-dish, dress with the melted butter flavoured with sage, and sprinkle with grated Grana.

Let the flavours blend for a few seconds before serving.

CREPES GRATIN

📷

For the crepes: 2.5 dl milk, 125 g flour, 2 eggs, 30 g butter, salt.

A dish of crepes on the table is always a welcome sight to the diners. They lend a touch of class to the simplest meals, and, contrary to popular belief, can be very easily prepared with a minimum of organisation.

The range of possible fillings is endless, including vegetables, cheese, meat or fish. Traditional recipes are given here, leaving the creation of more imaginative combinations to the inventive flair of each individual cook. All involve preparing the basic crepe batter and a béchamel sauce, which is used for binding the filling as well as for pouring over the finished dish.

The quantities given are sufficient for about 12 crepes. Melt the butter over low heat. Beat the eggs, flour and a pinch of salt with an egg-whisk, then, continuing to whisk, dilute with the milk and the melted butter.

Lightly oil and heat an 18-cm diameter non-stick frying pan. When the pan is hot, pour a ladleful of batter onto it. When the crepe is golden on one side, flip it over with a spatula and brown the other side. Continue until all the batter is used up.

These crepes can be prepared the day before and stored in the fridge covered with cling film.

WITH RED CHICORY FILLING

◆

600 g red chicory, 1 onion, béchamel (see page 141), grated Parmesan cheese, dry white wine, salt and pepper.

Wash and slice the onion and chicory, then sauté lightly in a saucepan with a little oil. Sprinkle the vegetables with white wine, season with salt and pepper, lower the heat and simmer for another ten minutes. Prepare the béchamel and mix half of it with the chicory and onion.

Fill the crepes with this mixture, then fold them in four and arrange slightly overlapping in a buttered ovenproof dish. Pour the rest of the béchamel

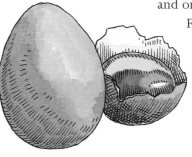

over them, sprinkle with grated Parmesan, and dot with bits of butter. Brown in a hot oven at 180 °C.

WITH SHELLFISH FILLING

◆

500 g prawns and scampi, 1 small lobster, 2 cloves garlic, 1 bunch parsley, 1/2 dose béchamel, (see page 141), cooking cream, 1/2 shot brandy, extra-virgin olive oil, butter, salt and pepper.

Wash the prawns and scampi, remove the shells and sauté for 5-6 minutes in a frying-pan with a tablespoon of butter. Prepare a shellfish stock with the shells and the lobster. Drain the lobster when done and remove the flesh, then strain the cooking juices and set aside.

In a saucepan, sauté the garlic cloves in a few tablespoons of oil; as soon as they begin to brown, remove them and add the finely chopped shellfish meat. Stir gently, letting the flavours blend. Pour in the brandy and when it has almost all evaporated, add a few spoonfuls of the fish stock thickened with a little flour. Let the sauce reduce; add salt and pepper to taste before removing from the heat.

Prepare the béchamel (you can even use the lobster fumet instead of milk) and as soon as it begins to boil, add a little chopped parsley and dilute with the cream. Continue cooking, stirring constantly, until the sauce has reached the right consistency (which should be rather more liquid than a normal béchamel).

Place a spoonful of the fish sauce at the centre of each crepe, fold in four, then arrange them slightly overlapping in a buttered ovenproof dish. Pour the béchamel over the crepes and dot with a few flakes of butter. Brown in a hot oven (200 °C) for about 10 minutes before serving.

POTATO CULINGIONIS

📷

For the pasta: *500 g white flour, water.*
For the filling: *600 g potatoes, 1 onion, 2 cloves garlic, fresh mint, 300 g grated aged pecorino cheese, extra-virgin olive oil, salt.*
For the sauce: *tomato sauce (see page 143).*

In a bowl or on a floured surface, mix the flour with enough warm water to form a smooth, elastic dough. Add a little salt and knead thoroughly. Shape into a ball, cover with a clean teacloth and leave to rise.

In the meantime, peel, wash and boil the potatoes, then mash them in a bowl with the grated pecorino and a pinch of salt. Peel and chop the onion and garlic and a few mint leaves, sauté in a little oil for a few minutes (preferably in an earthenware pot), then add to the potato mixture and mix well. When the mixture is thoroughly blended, roll it into small balls.

Roll the pasta into two thin sheets. Arrange the potato balls at equal distances over one of the sheets. Place the other sheet of pasta on top, press down with your fingertips in the spaces between the filled sections, and cut out with a

pastry wheel, sealing the edges well. Boil in plenty of salted water, then drain and dress with tomato sauce (or melted butter if preferred). Before serving, sprinkle generously with grated pecorino.

FLORENTINE GNOCCHI

◆

1 kg potatoes, 300 g spinach, 200 g white flour, 1 egg, a few sage leaves, butter, grated Parmesan cheese, salt.

Peel the potatoes and boil them in salted water. Cook the spinach in a little boiling water, squeeze thoroughly and pass through a sieve. Mash the potatoes, add the spinach, and bind them together with a beaten egg. Stir in the flour, adding more if the mixture seems too soft. Roll out into long sausages, cut them into lengths of about 2 cm, and place them on a floured teacloth. Bring a large pot of salted water to the boil and drop in the gnocchi, removing them with a slotted spoon as soon as they come to the surface. Melt the butter, flavouring it with the sage, and pour it over the gnocchi on a serving-dish. Sprinkle generously with grated Parmesan.

SPINACH GNOCCHI

◆

1 kg spinach, 350 g ricotta cheese, 2 egg yolks, grated Parmesan cheese, flour, a few sage leaves, butter, grated nutmeg, salt and pepper.

Clean the spinach well; boil it in a little salted water, drain and squeeze thoroughly, then chop finely. In a bowl, mash the ricotta with a fork, add the spinach, and bind together with the egg yolks and 1 1/2 tablespoons of Parmesan, seasoning with salt, pepper and grated nutmeg.
With the help of a teaspoon, shape the mixture into balls about the size of a walnut and roll them in flour, then drop them into a large pot of boiling salted water.
As soon as they come to the surface, remove them carefully with a slotted spoon. Serve with melted butter flavoured with sage and sprinkled with grated Parmesan.

VALLE D'AOSTA GNOCCHI

◆

200 g coarse cornmeal, 100 g fine cornmeal, 150 g Fontina cheese, 2 egg yolks, 1 l milk, grated nutmeg, grated Parmesan cheese, butter, salt and pepper.

Pour the milk into a saucepan and heat. When it is about to boil, pour in the two types of cornmeal and a pinch of salt, then beat with an egg-whisk.

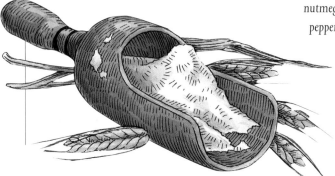

Continue cooking like a normal corn-meal, stirring occasionally. When it is done, after about 40 minutes, stir in the diced Fontina, 2 teaspoons of butter and a pinch of grated nutmeg. Let it cool slightly, then blend in the two egg yolks and roll out about 1 cm thick on a floured surface.

When it has cooled, use a glass to cut out disks of about 4 or 5 cm. Lay the disks overlapping in a buttered oven-proof dish.

Sprinkle with grated Parmesan and pepper, pour over the melted butter, and brown in a hot oven for about 10 minutes before serving.

PRUNE GNOCCHI

◆

1 kg potatoes, 1 kg dried prunes, 200 g white flour, 1 egg, 30 g butter, sugar as required, salt.

With the above ingredients (except of course the prunes and the sugar) prepare a mixture for normal potato gnocchi, but make it into large gnocchi about twice the usual size.

Make a hollow in each one with your fingers, and insert a pitted prune which has a teaspoon of sugar replacing the pit.

A useful guide is to have about the same amount of potatoes and prunes in each of the gnocchi. Bring a large pot of salted water to the boil and drop in the gnocchi. From the moment they rise to the surface, calculate about 15 minutes cooking time.

The unique feature of this traditional Trieste dish is that it can be served as a first course, garnished with bread-crumbs lightly fried in butter; as a second course to accompany game; or as a dessert, dressed with melted butter and sprinkled with sugar and cinnamon to taste.

POTATO GNOCCHI WITH TOMATOES

◆

1 kg potatoes, 200 g white flour, 500 g tomato pulp, 1 onion, a few sage leaves, butter, salt and pepper.

Boil the potatoes in their skins, then peel and mash them while still hot. Place the mashed potatoes on a floured surface; lightly incorporate the salt and enough flour to produce the right consistency. (Soft, fluffy gnocchi are made by using only a little flour and are ideally floury "gnocchi potatoes").

Roll the mixture into finger-size sausages, cut into pieces, and give them the typical gnocchi shape by lightly pushing them against the back of a fork.

Prepare the sauce: put the tomato pulp and the onion, cut into wedges, into a large saucepan with a tablespoon of butter, salt and pepper. Cook over moderate heat for about 15 minutes, then switch off and remove the onions.

Bring a large pot of salted water to the boil and drop in the gnocchi a few at a time. As soon as they rise to the surface, remove with a slotted spoon and serve directly on the dinner plates, spooning

FISH FUMET (STOCK)

250 g fish scraps or mixed second-rate fish, 1 onion, 1 carrot, 1 celery stalk, bay leaves, sage, thyme, juniper berries, 1 large slice of lemon, a little white wine, salt, peppercorns.

Put the fish in a large pot with 2 litres of water, the onion cut into wedges, the coarsely chopped celery and carrot, the herbs, a handful of salt, a few peppercorns, the lemon and the wine. Bring to the boil over moderate heat, skimming frequently, then simmer for about 40 minutes. Strain the fish stock thoroughly before use. It can also be enriched by adding the puréed fish meat.

the tomato sauce over. Serve the grated Parmesan separately.

Gnocchi make an excellent first course, and can be served with various sauces: tomato, meat sauce, pesto, a sauce made with four different kinds of cheese or simply with butter browned with a few sage leaves.

FISH GNOCCHI

◆

600 g potatoes, 300 g fillets of sole (or other delicate fish), 2 anchovy fillets in oil, 400 g tomato pulp, 1 bunch herbs (sage, rosemary, marjoram), 1 shallot, 1 onion, 1 clove garlic, 2 teaspoons olive paste, 1 egg, about 150 g white flour, dry white wine, extra-virgin olive oil, salt and pepper.

Chop the garlic and onion very finely and sauté in 1 1/2 tablespoons of oil, then add the fish cut into pieces and let the flavours blend for a few minutes. Pour in the white wine; when it has al-

most entirely evaporated, season with salt and pepper and leave on the heat for a few more minutes. Let cool, then blend in the blender.

Boil the potatoes in salted water. Peel while still hot, mash, and place on a floured surface. Make a well in the centre, break the egg into it and add the fish. Blend all the ingredients thoroughly, adding the flour gradually, and knead into a smooth paste of the right consistency.

Keeping the gnocchi mixture warm, prepare the sauce. In a saucepan, sauté the finely chopped shallot in a little oil. Add the anchovies and stir until they disintegrate.

Add the olive paste, the chopped tomato pulp, salt and pepper, and cook for five minutes, stirring in the chopped herbs just before removing the pan from the heat.

Roll the gnocchi paste into long sausages and cut into short lengths. Use the prongs of a fork to give them the typical gnocchi shape, or rub them over the back of a fork or a grater.

Bring a large pot of salted water to the boil and drop in the gnocchi a few at a time.

Remove with a slotted spoon as soon as they come to the surface. Serve with the tomato and anchovy sauce.

RICOTTA GNOCCHI

◆

400 g fresh ricotta cheese, 300 g white flour, breadcrumbs, 2 eggs, grated Parmesan cheese, a few sage leaves, extra-virgin olive oil, butter, ginger, nutmeg, salt.

Put the ricotta in a bowl and beat vigorously with a wooden spoon until creamy. Add 2 or 3 tablespoons of oil, the eggs, a pinch of salt, 2 tablespoons of grated Parmesan, a pinch of freshly grated ginger and one of nutmeg. Stir in the flour, and enough breadcrumbs to stiffen the mixture sufficiently. Blend thoroughly, then refrigerate for half an hour. Roll the cooled mixture into long sausages and cut them into gnocchi of the desired length.

Boil in abundant salted water and drain, a few at a time, with a slotted spoon. Serve the gnocchi dressed with the melted butter (flavoured with sage) and sprinkled generously with grated Parmesan.

SEMOLINA GNOCCHI

◆

250 g semolina, 1 l milk, 2 egg yolks, 150 g butter, 100 g grated Parmesan cheese, a few sage leaves, grated nutmeg, salt.

Pour the milk and half a litre of water into a large pot with a pinch of salt. Heat, and when it begins to boil, sprinkle in the semolina, beating constantly to avoid lumps.

Cook for about ten minutes, remove from the heat and let cool slightly. Then stir in the egg yolks, a pinch of nutmeg and a little Parmesan, blending thoroughly. Pour the mixture onto a counter (preferably marble), spread about 1 cm thick using a spatula, then let cool.

Using a special cutter, or a glass with moistened rim, cut into circles (or if you prefer, ovals) and arrange slightly overlapping in a buttered ovenproof dish. Sprinkle generously with grated Parmesan and a few chopped sage leaves, dot with flakes of butter and brown in a hot oven (200 °C) for about 15 minutes.

PUMPKIN GNOCCHI

◆

1.5 kg sweet yellow pumpkin, 250 g white flour, 2 eggs, 150 g grated Parmesan cheese, 100 g butter, ginger, salt, ground hot red pepper.

Peel the pumpkin and remove the seeds, then boil it in water or steam it.

When the pumpkin is done, drain and mash it. Put it in a bowl with the flour, eggs, a pinch of salt, a pinch of hot red pepper and one of freshly grated ginger. Blend all the ingredients well to form a paste, then roll out into long sausages and cut into gnocchi-length pieces, around 2 cm.

Drop a few at a time into a large saucepan of lightly salted water, removing them with a slotted spoon as soon as they come to the surface.

Place them in a serving-dish, dress them with the melted butter and sprinkle with grated Parmesan.

GNOCCHI
GRATIN
📷

1 kg potatoes, 3 eggs, 1 cup béchamel (see page 141), 2 1/2 tablespoons of table cream, grated Parmesan cheese, 80 g butter, salt.

Choose suitable floury potatoes. Boil them, then peel and mash them while still hot. Stir in the salt, 2 eggs, 50 g butter and 2 tablespoons of grated Parmesan, blending thoroughly.

Spread the mixture on a buttered surface, levelling it out about 1 cm thick, and let it cool. Then cut out disks, using a special cutter or a glass with moistened rim.

Prepare the béchamel according to the basic recipe. Butter an ovenproof dish and arrange the gnocchi in layers, covering each layer with béchamel and grated Parmesan. Brown in a hot oven for about 10 minutes.

LANGAROLI
◆

For the pasta: *(recipe on page 138).*
For the filling: *100 g boiled beef, 50 g boiled rice, 50 g white cabbage, 50 g grated aged Toma d'Alba cheese, 2 eggs, grated nutmeg, butter, salt and pepper.*
For the sauce: *150 g ground leg of veal, 2 ripe and firm tomatoes, 1 leek, 1 sprig rosemary, grated Parmesan cheese, extra-virgin olive oil, salt and pepper.*

Wash and dry the cabbage leaves, shred them and sauté them in a saucepan with the butter. Add the minced boiled beef, season with salt, pepper and nutmeg, and brown it while stirring for a few minutes. Remove from the heat and let cool. Adding the eggs, the boiled rice and the grated Toma d'Alba. Blend all the ingredients thoroughly.

Roll out the pasta into two thin sheets. On one, place teaspoonfuls of the filling at equal distances. Cover with the second sheet of pasta, then press with your fingertips around each filled section. With a knife, cut the pasta into squares of about 1.5 cm, then seal the edges by pinching them. Put the finely chopped leek into a saucepan with the rosemary, sauté lightly in oil, add the ground veal, and brown for a few minutes while stirring.

Blanch the tomatoes in boiling water, peel, seed, and chop them, then add them to the saucepan. Season the sauce with salt and pepper and let it reduce over moderate heat. Bring a large pot of salted water to the boil and cook the langaroli. Drain and pour into a warm serving-dish, dress with the meat sauce, and sprinkle with grated Parmesan before serving.

RAVIOLI

◆

For the pasta: (recipe on page 138).

Ravioli come in a wide variety of shapes and fillings. Different shapes of ravioli can be created by using the different pasta cutters available on the market. For the filling, you can either use the classic meat or ricotta stuffing or one of the three fillings suggested below.

The first step consists of making the pasta, following the basic recipe provided. When you have prepared the filling, roll the pasta into a thin sheet on a floured surface. Place small heaps of the filling on half of the sheet of pasta at equal distances. Fold over the other half of the sheet and use the special cutters to cut the ravioli into the desired shape.

A useful tip: brush the pasta between the filled sections with beaten egg white. This helps to bind the two layers when the edges of the ravioli are pressed together.

Leave the prepared ravioli in a cool place for about a day, then cook them in abundant salted water. Drain and serve with melted butter and grated Parmesan, or with a light tomato sauce, as desired.

WITH MUSHROOM FILLING

◆

250 g fresh ricotta cheese, 250 g fresh mushrooms, 1 clove garlic, 1 bunch parsley, grated Parmesan cheese, extra-virgin olive oil, salt and pepper.

Clean the mushrooms, removing the soil with a damp cloth, then slice them

and stew in a saucepan with a little oil and the crushed garlic clove. Before removing from the heat, season with salt, pepper and finely-chopped parsley.

Remove the garlic and chop the mushrooms very fine. In a bowl, mash the ricotta thoroughly with a fork, beating until it is creamy, add a little grated Parmesan, then stir in the mushroom mixture.

WITH FISH FILLING

◆

400 g boiled fish, 2 eggs, 2 teaspoons chopped pistachios, 120 g grated Parmesan cheese, a few sage leaves, butter or extra-virgin olive oil, grated nutmeg, salt.

Remove the skin and bones from the fish, chop it, then put it in a bowl with the grated Parmesan, the eggs, pistachios, salt, and a pinch of nutmeg. Blend these ingredients thoroughly.

Different types of fish may be used (trout, sturgeon etc.), providing a varied range of flavours. Dress the ravioli with cream and a little tomato sauce.

WITH ARTICHOKE FILLING

◆

5 artichokes, 1/2 onion, 1/2 clove garlic, 1 bunch parsley, 1 lemon, 80 g ricotta cheese, 2 tablespoons of grated Parmesan cheese, 2 eggs, extra-virgin olive oil, salt.

Clean the artichokes, removing most of the stalk, the tips and the tough outer leaves. Cut into wedges and soak in water mixed with lemon juice for half an hour. Chop the garlic and onion; sauté them until wilted in a saucepan with a little oil. Add the thinly sliced artichokes and simmer over moderate heat for 30-40 minutes, adding a little hot water every so often. Before removing from the heat, season with salt, pepper and chopped parsley. Let cool. In a bowl, blend the ricotta with the eggs, the grated Parmesan and a pinch of salt, then stir in the finely chopped artichokes and mix well.

REDFISH RAVIOLI

◆

For the pasta: (*recipe on page 138*).
For the filling: *400 g cleaned redfish, 1 bunch mixed herbs, 1 egg yolk, 1 clove garlic, 1 lemon, 2 teaspoons mascarpone cheese, extra-virgin olive oil, salt and pepper.*
For the sauce: *butter, chives.*

In a saucepan, sauté the crushed garlic in plenty of oil. As soon as it is golden, remove it and add the fish, seasoning with a pinch of salt and a little grated lemon zest. Let the flavours merge for a few minutes, then remove from the heat.
Chop the redfish and blend it carefully with the mascarpone, the finely-chopped mixed herbs, the egg yolk, salt and pepper.
Prepare the ravioli using the recommended dough. Roll out a thin layer of pasta, then cut out squares 5x5 cm with the special cutter or a pastry wheel.

Place a teaspoon of the filling at the centre of each square, then place another square on top, and press into the typical ravioli shape.
Boil the ravioli in plenty of salted water or stock (vegetable or fish), draining them while still al dente. Before serving, mix with the melted butter and sprinkle with chopped chives.

SOLE RAVIOLI

◆

For the pasta: (*recipe on page 138*).
For the filling: *200 g sole fillets, 150 g borage, 50 g ricotta cheese, 2 eggs, grated Parmesan cheese, butter, salt and pepper.*
For the sauce: *150 g shelled clams, 1 clove garlic, 1 bunch parsley, 1 cup tomato sauce.*

Blanch the borage in salted boiling water, drain, squeeze and chop. Sauté the sole in the butter, then mash it with a fork. Place the fish and the borage in a bowl, add the eggs, the ricotta, a pinch of salt, one of pepper and a handful of grated Parmesan cheese. Mix well with a wooden spoon.
Roll out the pasta into a thin sheet, place small heaps of the mixture at equal distances over half of it, then fold over the pasta. Press down firmly with your fin-

gertips around the filled sections. Using a pastry wheel, cut the pasta into squares of about 2.5 cm.

Soak the clams in salted water for at least half an hour, then place them to open in a covered frying pan over high heat. Remove the shells, strain the juices and set aside.

Chop the garlic and parsley finely and sauté lightly in oil, add the clams, the tomato sauce and the strained cooking juices, and continue cooking to reduce the liquid.

Cook the ravioli in plenty of boiling salted water, drain and pour into a serving-bowl. Dress with the clam sauce and serve.

ASPARAGUS RAVIOLONI

♦

For the pasta: (recipe on page 138).
For the filling: 250 g asparagus tips, 100 g fresh ricotta cheese, 100 g grated Parmesan cheese, 1 egg, salt and pepper.
For the sauce: 40 g butter, 1 sprig rosemary, grated Parmesan cheese.

Steam the asparagus tips and set about 20 of them aside for the sauce. Chop the rest and mix them in a bowl with the ricotta, the grated Parmesan and the egg, then season with salt and pepper.

Blend the mixture well, then place teaspoonfuls of it at equal distances over half the sheet of rolled-out pasta. Fold over the pasta, pressing down with your fingertips around the filled sections, then cut into squares of about 4 cm.

In a small saucepan, melt and lightly colour the butter, flavouring it with the rosemary. In another saucepan, lightly sauté the remaining 20 asparagus tips. Cook the ravioloni in plenty of boiling salted water, drain and pour into a serving dish. Dress with the melted butter, sprinkle with the asparagus tips and grated Parmesan, and serve.

SCALLOP RAVIOLONI

♦

For the pasta: (recipe on page 138).
For the filling: 30 scallops, 2 eggs, 50 g ricotta cheese, salt and pepper.
For the sauce: 1 ladle tomato sauce, 1 bunch parsley, a few basil leaves, 1 clove garlic, extra-virgin olive oil, salt.

Clean the scallops under running water. Put them in a covered pot over high heat until they open. Strain the cooking juices and set aside. Shell the scallops, eliminate the inedible parts and chop the white flesh and the coral roe. In a bowl, blend the chopped scallops with the ricotta, eggs, salt and pepper.

Arrange small heaps of the mixture over half the sheet of rolled-out pasta; fold it over, pressing down well with your fingertips between the filled sections, then cut into squares of about 4 cm.

Cook the ravioloni in plenty of salted water, drain well and transfer to a serving-bowl. Pour the sauce over them, garnish with a teaspoon of chopped basil and one of chopped parsley, then serve.

ZUCCHINI RAVIOLONI

📷

For the pasta: (recipe on page 138).
For the filling: 200 g zucchini, 150 g fresh ricotta cheese, grated Parmesan cheese, butter, grated nutmeg, salt and pepper.
For the sauce: 4 ripe and firm tomatoes, a few basil leaves, 1 leek, a few sage leaves, 40 g butter, extra-virgin olive oil, grated Parmesan cheese, salt and, pepper.

Clean the zucchini, slice them thinly and sauté lightly in a little butter, seasoning with salt and grated nutmeg. Pass them through a sieve. Place the pureed zucchini in a bowl with the ricotta and a handful of grated Parmesan.

Make the ravioloni by arranging heaps of the mixture about the size of a walnut over half the sheet of rolled-out pasta. Fold over the other half and press down with your fingertips around the filled sections, then use a pastry wheel to cut out squares of about 4 cm.

Chop the leek finely and sauté it in a little oil. Blanch the tomatoes in boiling water for a few minutes, peel, seed and chop them, and add them to the leek with a pinch of salt. Leave to reduce, and in another small saucepan melt the butter, flavouring it with a few sage leaves.

Cook the ravioloni in plenty of boiling salted water, drain well and transfer to a serving dish. Pour the tomato sauce and the melted butter over them and mix. Garnish with chopped basil, sprinkle with grated Parmesan, and serve.

CHIODINI MUSHROOM ROLL

◆

600 g potatoes, 250 g chiodini (honey-coloured agaric or armillaria mushrooms), 200 g white flour, 100 g thinly sliced Fontina cheese, 1 clove garlic, 1 egg, 1 glass stock, grated Parmesan cheese, 150 g butter, salt and pepper.

Let the potatoes boil. In the meantime, clean the mushrooms with a damp cloth to remove the earthy residue. Slice them finely and sauté in a frying pan with 40 g of butter and the crushed garlic clove. Add the hot stock, season with pepper and simmer for about 10 minutes.

Peel and mash the potatoes, then place them on a floured surface. Add the sifted flour, the egg and a pinch of salt and knead thoroughly to form a smooth, compact dough. Roll out into a rectangle about 1 cm thick; cover with the slices of Fontina and the mushroom sauce.

Roll up and wrap tightly in a cloth, tying it at both ends. Bring to the boil a large pot of salted water, immerse the roll and cook for half an hour.

When done, untie the cloth, place the roll on a serving dish and cut into slices. Melt the remaining butter, pour it over the roll, then sprinkle generously with Parmesan cheese.

Alternatively, dot the sliced roll with bits of butter and brown it quickly in the oven.

GAME RAVIOLONI

For the pasta: (recipe on page 138).
For the filling: 2 partridges, 2 slices smoked bacon, 50 g black truffle, 200 g spinach, 1 egg, 1 glass dry white wine, 1 sprig rosemary, grated Parmesan cheese, extra-virgin olive oil.
For the sauce: 40 g butter, 1 clove garlic, a few sage leaves, grated Parmesan cheese.

Clean, pluck and sear the partridges, and remove the entrails; wash thoroughly and dry. Wrap them in bacon and rosemary and brown them in the oil, sprinkling with white wine. When the wine has evaporated, lower the heat and cook until done, adding a few tablespoons of hot water from time to time if necessary. After about an hour, remove the partridges from the heat, debone them, and chop the meat. In another saucepan, blanch the spinach briefly in a little salted water, then drain, squeeze and chop it.
In a bowl, mix together the meat, spinach, egg, a generous handful of grated Parmesan, the truffle (cleaned and cut in flakes), and season with salt and pepper. Arrange small heaps of the mixture over half the sheet of rolled-out pasta; fold it over, pressing down well with your fingertips between the filled sections, then cut into squares of about 4 cm.
In a small saucepan, melt and lightly colour the butter, flavouring it with a clove of garlic and few leaves of sage. Cook the ravioloni in plenty of boiling salted water, drain and transfer to a serving dish. Remove the garlic and

rosemary from the melted butter and pour it over the ravioloni. Sprinkle generously with grated Parmesan and serve.

STROZZAPRETI WITH OX MARROW

For the pasta: 200 g white flour, 200 g whole-grain flour, 2 eggs, 300 g spinach, salt.
For the sauce: 150 g ground leg of veal, 80 g ox marrow, 1 small onion, 1 celery stalk, 1/2 carrot, 1 sprig rosemary, 2 bay leaves, 1 cup tomato purée, 1 glass vegetable stock, 1 glass dry white wine, grated Parmesan cheese, extra-virgin olive oil, salt and pepper.

Boil the spinach in a little salted water, squeeze it dry and purée in the blender. Mix the two kinds of flour in a heap on the work-surface. Make a well in the centre, break in the eggs, then add a pinch of salt and the spinach purée. Knead thoroughly with your hands to form a smooth, elastic dough. Cover the pasta with a damp teacloth, set aside for 15 minutes, then knead again. With well-floured fingers, break off pieces of dough about the size of a hazelnut, shaping them into slightly elongated gnocchi.
Chop the carrot, celery, onion and rosemary finely. Sauté them in a saucepan with oil, adding the bay leaf, a pinch of salt and one of pepper. Add the ground meat and ox marrow and brown for a few minutes, stirring constantly. Then pour over the white wine and let it evaporate. Lower the heat, add the tomato purée and simmer over low heat,

124

adding a little hot vegetable stock from time to time. Cook the strozzapreti in plenty of boiling salted water, drain, pour them into the pan with the sauce, and mix well. Add a generous handful of grated Parmesan and serve.

SPINACH ROLL

◆

For the pasta: 250 g white flour, 2 eggs, 2 tea-spoons extra-virgin olive oil, salt.
For the filling: 600 g spinach, 150 g fresh ricot-ta cheese, 100 g grated Parmesan cheese, 1 egg, ground hot red pepper, extra-virgin olive oil, salt.
For the sauce: tomato sauce, grated Parmesan cheese.

Wash the spinach carefully, steam it or boil it in a little salted water, then chop finely. In a bowl, mash the ricotta with a fork; add the spinach, grated Parmesan and egg. Season with salt and a pinch of hot red pepper, then cover the bowl and refrigerate. In the meantime, pile the flour onto a floured surface, make a well in the centre and break in the eggs, adding a tiny amount of water, the oil and the salt. Work thoroughly with your fingertips, then knead with the palms of the hands until the dough is smooth, soft and elastic. Using a floured rolling-pin, roll the dough into a large, fairly thin rectangle, spread it with the pre-pared filling and roll it up, sealing the outer edges well.
Wrap the roll in a clean cloth, tying the ends carefully. Cook in a large pot of boiling salted water for about an hour. Serve with the tomato sauce poured over it and sprinkled with grated Parmesan.

STRANGOLAPRETI

300 g spinach, 2 stale bread rolls, 3 1/2 table-spoons white flour, 2 eggs, milk, a few sage leaves, grated Parmesan cheese, butter, salt.

Strangolapreti is a typical Alto Adige dish, which can also be made with net-tles, spinach beet or wild spinach.
Clean the spinach carefully, wash it, and steam or cook in a small amount of boiling water, then drain, squeeze and chop finely.
In the meantime, crumble the bread into a bowl, moistening it with a little milk.
Add the eggs, the flour and a pinch of salt and mix well. Lastly, add the spin-ach and shape the mixture into gnocchi about the size of a large walnut.
Bring a large pot of salted water to the boil and cook the gnocchi until they come to the surface. It's best to cook the gnocchi a few at a time, to keep them from sticking together.
Drain carefully, then dress with the melted butter, flavoured with a few sage leaves and the grated cheese.

AUBERGINE TORTELLINI

◆

For the pasta: (recipe on page 138).
For the filling: 200 g aubergines, 300 g ricotta cheese, a few walnuts, a few sage leaves, 1 bunch parsley, grated Parmesan cheese, extra-virgin olive oil, salt.
For the sauce: tomato sauce, grated Parmesan cheese.

Prepare the pasta according to the basic recipe. Slice the aubergines, sprinkle with sea-salt, and leave for about half an hour for the water to drain off. Dry the slices, place them in an oiled oven-proof dish, and brown both sides in the oven. Remove the dish from the oven, let it cool, then chop the aubergines with a half-moon chopper. Place them in a bowl with the ricotta, the chopped walnuts, a little Parmesan, a handful of chopped parsley and a few chopped sage leaves, and mix well.

Cut the pastry into squares. Place a small heap of the filling on each, then fold over, seal and shape into tortellini. Cook in plenty of salted water or in vegetable stock. Dress with tomato sauce and sprinkle with Parmesan cheese.

128

POTATO AND SPINACH STRUDEL

◆

1 kg potatoes, 1 kg spinach, 400 g white flour, 1 egg, grated Grana cheese, butter, salt.

Start by washing the potatoes and boiling them in their skins. In the meantime, clean and wash the spinach and either steam or cook it in a little salted water. When the potatoes are done, peel and mash them before blending them with the flour, the egg and a pinch of salt. Roll out the pasta about one centimetre thick on a clean, damp tea-cloth. Cover it with the

spinach, lightly tossed in a little melted butter, then roll it up and wrap it in a clean tea cloth. Tie the ends of the roll carefully with kitchen thread. Cook in a large pot of boiling salted water for about an hour. When the strugolo is done, remove the teacloth and slice it. Cover the slices with a good meat sauce and sprinkle with grated Grana cheese.

CHICKPEA TORTELLI

◆

For the pasta: (recipe on page 138).
For the filling: 150 g chickpeas, 1 onion, extra-virgin olive oil, salt.
For the sauce: a few sage leaves, grated Parmesan cheese, butter.

Prepare the pasta by the basic recipe. If you are using dried chickpeas, soak them overnight in cold water. Cook the chickpeas in boiling water, drain, and purée them in a food-mill. Slice the onion and stew in a lightly-oiled saucepan; add the chickpea purée, salt, and let the flavours blend. Remove from the heat and add enough oil to make a soft paste. Cut the pasta into squares. Place a small heap of the chick pea mixture in the middle of each square, sealing and shaping them in the normal way. Cook the tortelli in a large pot of boiling salted water. Sauté the chopped sage in plenty of butter, and use it to season the drained tortelli. Sprinkle with grated Parmesan and serve.

PUMPKIN TORTELLI

◆

40 g white flour, 1 kg bumpy yellow pumpkin, 100 g macaroons, 150 g grated Parmesan cheese, 5 eggs, butter, grated nutmeg, a few sage leaves, salt.

Remove the rind and seeds from the pumpkin and cook it in the oven. Sieve the pulp into a bowl and blend in one egg, the crumbled macaroons and the grated Parmesan, seasoning with salt and nutmeg. Mix the flour with the remaining eggs and a pinch of salt, kneading well until you have a firm, even dough. Roll out into a thin sheet, then cut it into squares. Place a little of the pumpkin filling at the centre of each, then fold over the pasta, sealing the edges well.

Melt the butter, flavouring it with a few sage leaves. Cook the tortelli in plenty of boiling salted water, drain, and serve-dressed with the flavoured butter and sprinkled with grated Parmesan.

In Lombardy, this filling is made with the addition of about 100 g of Cremona mustard (candied fruit in a mustard syrup), with the fruit chopped in the syrup.

TORTELLINI
WITH MEAT FILLING

◆

For the pasta: (recipe on page 138).
For the filling: 100 g chicken breast, 100 g pork loin, 100 g veal, 150 g Parma ham, 1 fairly thick slice Mortadella sausage, 100 g grated Parmesan cheese, 2 eggs, butter, nutmeg, salt and pepper.

Grind the meat and brown in a saucepan with a tablespoon of butter, then place it in a bowl with the chopped ham and chopped mortadella. Blend together with the 2 eggs, add the grated Parmesan and season with a pinch of grated nutmeg, salt and pepper.

Make the pasta following the basic recipe. Roll it into a thin sheet, cut it into squares of about 4-5 cm (as you become more expert, you will be able to make even smaller tortellini) and heap a little of the filling on each one. Fold the opposite corners together to form a triangle, seal the edges well, then roll it around your finger and pinch the two ends together, turning the upper edge outwards.

Cook the tortellini in boiling salted water, or better still in hot meat stock. Drain and serve with a meat sauce, or if you prefer simply with melted butter flavoured with a few sage leaves.

TORTELLONI
WITH VEGETARIAN FILLING

◆

For the pasta: (recipe on page 138).
For the filling: 350 g spinach beet, 250 g ricotta cheese, salt and pepper.
For the sauce: a few sage leaves, grated Parmesan cheese, butter.

Prepare the pasta by the basic recipe. Trim the spinach beet and boil in a little salted water, then chop and place in a bowl with the ricotta, which has been beaten into a smooth cream. Blend well, season with salt and pepper.

Roll the pasta into a thin sheet. Place the filling in small heaps at equal distances over half the pasta. Fold over the other half, then cut the tortelloni into the desired shape using the special cutters; seal the edges well. Cook the tortelloni in plenty of boiling water, drain, and transfer to a serving dish. Pour over them the melted butter, flavoured with a few sage leaves, and sprinkle with grated Parmesan. These tortelloni are also excellent served with a light tomato sauce.

POTATO TORTELLONI

◆

For the pasta: 500 g wheat flour, 200 g floury potatoes, 3 eggs, salt.
For the filling: 400 g mixed cheese (ricotta, Gorgonzola, Emmental etc.).
For the sauce: grated Parmesan cheese, butter.

Boil the potatoes, peel and mash them, then mix them with the flour. Blend in the eggs, a pinch of salt and a little of the potato cooking water, and knead into a pliable dough. Roll flat on a floured surface and cut into strips of about 10 cm. In the lower half of each strip, place small heaps of the finely-diced cheeses at equal distances. Fold over the top half of the strip, pressing the edges down well. Cut out

the tortelloni using the special cutter, or a glass with lightly moistened rim. Bring a large pot of salted water to the boil, drop in the tortelloni and cook briefly. Drain and transfer to a warm serving-dish, dress with the melted butter, sprinkle with grated Parmesan, and serve.

TORTELLONI WITH SPINACH AND RICOTTA FILLING

For the pasta: (recipe on page 138).
For the filling: 300 g spinach, 300 g ricotta cheese, 1 bunch parsley, 2 eggs, grated nutmeg, 50 g grated Parmesan cheese, salt and pepper.
For the sauce: a few sage leaves, 100 g grated Parmesan cheese, butter.

Prepare the pasta following the basic recipe.
Pass the ricotta through a sieve. Boil the spinach in a little salted water, drain, squeeze thoroughly and chop. Place the ricotta and spinach in a bowl; blend in the eggs, chopped parsley and grated Parmesan, seasoning the mixture with salt, pepper and a pinch of grated nutmeg. Mix all of the ingredients to form a smooth cream.
Roll the pasta into a thin sheet and cut out disks of about 8 cm. Place a small heap of filling at the centre of each disk, then fold in half to form half-moon shapes, sealing the edges well. Cook in plenty of boiling salted water. When done, drain, and dress with the melted butter flavoured with a few sage leaves. Sprinkle generously with grated Parmesan and serve immediately.

Home made *pasta*

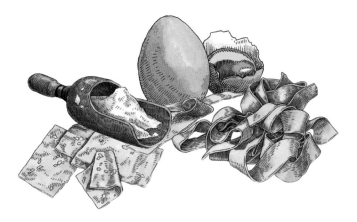

HOW TO COLOUR FRESH PASTA

If you want to make coloured pasta, here are a few suggestions:

- **yellow:** add a pinch of powdered saffron to the dough;
- **orange:** make the dough using only two eggs, and adding 400 g yellow pumpkin prepared as follows – peel, seed and steam the pumpkin, then sieve the pulp, drying it in a saucepan over the heat if it is too watery;
- **red:** make the dough using only 3 eggs and adding 2 tablespoons of tomato concentrate diluted in a little water;
- **green:** make the dough using only 2 eggs and adding 200 g of boiled, squeezed and finely-chopped spinach.
- **brown:** add 50-60 g unsweetened cocoa powder to the dough;
- **black:** make the dough using only 3 eggs and add the strained contents of 2 cuttlefish ink sacs diluted in a little white wine.

PASTA WITHOUT EGGS

CAVATIEDDI
◆

200 g extra-fine flour, 100 g wheat flour, water, salt.

Mix the two types of flour and pour them onto a floured surface, then blend well with a pinch of salt dissolved in a little warm water.

Knead thoroughly to form a smooth, soft dough, then roll into long sausages about 1/2 cm thick, and cut into maccheroni-length pieces.

As you cut the pieces, drag a round-bladed knife across each piece to slightly flatten and curl the pasta into elongated shell shapes. Then lay them out to dry on a floured teacloth.

Cavatieddi is a pasta typical of Sicily.

FETTUCCINE
◆

400 g durum wheat flour, 10 g extra-virgin olive oil, water, salt.

Pour the flour onto a cutting board, make a well in the middle and pour in the oil, a little warm water and a pinch of salt. Knead vigorously, adding more water gradually as required. Roll into a ball and set aside for half an hour.

Roll out the pasta as thin as possible and leave it to dry, covered with a teacloth, on a wooden board, then cut it into fettucine strips about 1 cm wide.

HOW TO COOK FRESH PASTA

Fresh pasta must be cooked in plenty of salted water. The recommended amount of water is about eight times the weight of the pasta. A spoonful of oil added to the water keeps the pasta from sticking together. It is essential to drop in the pasta when the water is already boiling, stirring gently with a wooden fork so that it does not stick to the bottom or stick together in lumps.

Filled pasta should, on the other hand, be dropped into the water just before it comes to the boil, to keep the shapes from opening and the filling from spilling out.

When you drop in the pasta, the water stops boiling, so you must turn up the heat to bring it back to the boil. Once the water is boiling again, adjust the heat so that it continues to boil gently. Never cover the boiling pot completely, or the water will boil over. Cooking times depend on the type of pasta, the thickness, the various ingredients used (egg, different types of flour, etc), and on individual taste. However, we recommend draining the pasta while it still has 'bite' or is, as the Italians say, al dente.

Filled pasta should be cooked with special care, because if cooked too long or over too high a heat, the pasta shapes may split or break open.

It is also important that the water used for cooking the pasta is not too calcareous, since hard water can obstruct the natural porosity of the pasta so that it does not cook evenly. This problem can be easily solved by fitting the water supply with a special filter.

MALLOREDDUS

◆

400 g durum wheat flour, white flour as required, 1 pinch saffron, water, salt.

Dissolve the saffron and the salt in a cup of water, and blend this into the wheat flour on a floured surface.

Knead the pasta, adding as much white flour as necessary to form a soft, smooth dough.

Roll the pasta out into long sausages about 1/2 cm thick and cut into 2-cm lengths.

Malloreddus are traditionally marked using a special bamboo tool, but if you haven't got one you can press them against the back of a fork like gnocchi to produce a similar effect, they shoul look like little shells.

Then leave them to dry on floured tea-cloths in a fairly cool place.

ORECCHIETTE

◆

160 g extra-fine flour, 240 g durum wheat flour, water, salt.

Mix the two flours on a breadboard and make a mound with a well in the centre. Add a pinch of salt and enough water to mix and knead into a smooth, elastic dough.

Knead thoroughly for about 10 minutes until the water is absorbed, then roll the dough out into long sausages and cut into pieces about 1 cm long.

Using a round-bladed knife, flatten each cylinder into a shell-shape on a floured breadboard, then form into 'little ears' by moulding them over the tip of your thumb. Leave them to dry on lightly floured teacloths.

Orecchiette is a pasta typical of Puglia (a southern region of Italy).

PICI

◆

400 g extra-fine flour, extra-virgin olive oil, water, salt.

This typical Sienese pasta is a kind of homemade spaghetti. Pici are made by hand and rolled out on a breadboard, and the most expert housewives can roll them up to two metres long!

Heap the flour at the centre of the breadboard, add 2 teaspoons of extra-virgin olive oil, a pinch of salt, and enough water to mix the dough. Knead energetically, adding a little warm water gradually if required.

When you have a firm, smooth dough, roll it into a ball, brush the surface with oil, and let it rest, covered with a tea-cloth, for about half an hour.

Then roll it into a sheet about 1.5 cm thick and cut into thin 3 mm strips, rolling them with

HOW TO STORE FRESH PASTA

Store in the fridge. The ideal temperature for fresh and filled pasta is 3 or 4 °C. Don't cover it with cling film or keep it closed in plastic containers, since pasta has to 'breathe'. It is best stored in special paper or cardboard food containers, or better still on a ceramic plate covered with a cotton cloth.

Out of the fridge. We strongly advise against storing pasta out of the fridge, especially filled pasta, since high temperatures or changes in temperature can accelerate the deterioration of the ingredients. Moreover, in the case of filled pasta, the fats in the filling will tend to leak out onto the pasta case.

well-floured hands into the shape of spaghetti.

As you prepare the pici, place them to dry on a teacloth dusted with flour or semolina to keep them from sticking together.

PISAREI

◆

300 g extra-fine flour, 100 g breadcrumbs, water, salt.

Blanch the breadcrumbs in a little boiling water, then blend with the flour on the breadboard, adding a pinch of salt and enough water to mix the dough. Knead thoroughly until you have a firm, smooth, elastic dough.

Divide the dough into balls. Roll the balls out into sausages about 1/2 cm thick, then cut into pieces about 1.5 cm long. Use your thumb to mould the cylinders into shell-shapes.

PIZZOCCHERI

◆

250 g buckwheat flour, 150 g extra-fine flour, water, salt and pepper.

Mix the two kinds of flours on a floured breadboard and make a mound with a well in the centre. Add a pinch of salt and enough water to blend.

Knead thoroughly until you have a firm, elastic dough. With a rolling-pin, roll out a sheet about 1.5 mm thick, and cut into strips about 1 cm wide and 7 cm long.

SPAGHETTI ALLA CHITARRA

◆

400 g extra-fine flour, 1 1/2 tablespoons lard, water, salt.

Cut the lard into the flour, adding salt and enough water to make a firm, elastic dough.

Knead thoroughly, then roll out a sheet as large as the frame of the wooden 'guitar' tool.

The chitarra, or guitar, is an instrument consisting of a wooden frame strung with wires, used for cutting spaghetti. The sheet of pasta is laid on top, then pressed through by rolling over it with the rolling pin.

If you do not have a 'guitar', use the draw-plate of the pasta machine that is normally used for tagliolini. When you have finished, place the spaghetti on a floured teacloth to dry.

TROFIE

◆

400 g extra-fine flour, water, salt.

Pour the flour onto the breadboard, add a pinch of salt and enough water to mix. Knead thoroughly with your hands until you have a dense, smooth, elastic dough.

Break off pieces about the size of a bean, roll them into thin sausages, then, with well-floured hands, twist them into corkscrew shapes. Leave them to dry on a flour-sprinkled teacloth for four hours before cooking.

EGG PASTA

BIGOLI

◆

250 g extra-fine flour, 150 g durum wheat flour, 4 eggs, water, salt.

Pile the two kinds of flour in the middle of the breadboard, make a well in the centre, break the eggs into it and add a pinch of salt. Work the eggs into the flour, adding a little water if the mixture is too dry. Knead thoroughly to form a smooth, elastic dough. Put the dough through the pasta mill, using a wheel with 3 mm holes, then cut the bigoli into lengths of 20 cm with a knife. Leave the pasta to dry on a floured teacloth for several hours before using.

FILATIEDDI

◆

400 g extra-fine flour, 4 eggs, 2 teaspoons extra-virgin olive oil, salt.

Pour the flour into a heap on the breadboard. Make a well in the centre, add a pinch of salt and the oil, break in the eggs and beat with a fork. Knead thoroughly to form a firm dough. Shape it into a ball, wrap it in a tea cloth, moistened in warm water and well-wrung, and set aside for half an hour.
Roll the pasta with the rolling-pin into two sheets. Cut the sheets of pasta into squares, then shape them with your fingers into little wheels. As you prepare them, place them on a floured tray to rest for a few minutes.

GARGANELLI

◆

250 g extra-fine flour, 150 g durum wheat flour, 2 whole eggs and 1 yolk, salt.

Mix the two types of flour on the breadboard. Make a well in the centre and break in 2 whole eggs and 1 yolk along with a pinch of salt. Mix thoroughly and knead until you have a smooth, elastic dough.
Use a rolling-pin and roll out a sheet about 1 mm thick, then cut it into 6 cm squares. Roll these up diagonally around a wooden stick about the size of a pencil, pressing them with your fingertips. Then mark the garganelli using the special tool known as a comb, remove them, and lay them out to dry.

PASTA BASE
FOR CANNELLONI

◆

500 g extra-fine flour, 4 eggs, 2 teaspoons extra-virgin olive oil, salt.

Mound the flour onto the breadboard, make a well in the centre and break in the eggs, adding a pinch of salt and 2 teaspoons of extra-virgin olive oil. Rub in well, then knead to form a smooth, elastic dough. Leave covered in a damp teacloth for about half an hour, then knead again.
With a rolling-pin, roll out sheets about 1 mm thick. Use a knife to cut the pasta into squares of about 12 cm.

Cook the squares of pasta a few at a time, draining them while still al dente. Lay them out singly on a damp tea cloth to dry.

PASTA BASE
FOR LASAGNE

◆

500 g extra-fine flour, 4 eggs, 2 teaspoons extra-virgin olive oil, salt.

Add the eggs to the flour along with a pinch of salt and 2 teaspoons of extra-virgin olive oil. Mix well, then knead thoroughly with your hands to form a smooth, elastic dough. Leave the dough covered with a damp teacloth for about half an hour, then knead it again and roll out a sheet about 1.5 mm thick. Leave to rest for about 15 minutes, then use a knife to cut out squares of about 10 cm (the size varies according to requirements).

Let the squares of pasta dry for at least a couple of hours before cooking. Cook the lasagne a few at a time, draining them while al dente, and laying them out singly on a damp teacloth to dry.

PASTA BASE
FOR FRESH FILLED PASTA

◆

400 g extra-fine flour, 4 eggs, 2 teaspoons extra-virgin olive oil, salt.

Pour the flour onto the bread-board, make a well in the centre, break in the eggs, adding a pinch of salt and the oil. Mix thoroughly, kneading until you have a smooth, elastic dough. Leave covered with a damp tea-cloth for about half an hour, then knead again and roll out in thin sheets with the rolling-pin.

This pasta is much easier to work with if it is not allowed to dry out.

TAGLIATELLE,
TAGLIOLINI, FETTUCCINE,
PAPPARDELLE

◆

500 g extra-fine flour, 4 eggs, 2 teaspoons extra-virgin olive oil, 1 handful cornmeal.

Pour the flour in a heap onto a bread-board. Make a well in the centre, add the eggs with a pinch of salt and the oil. Blend in well and knead thoroughly with your hands until you have a smooth, elastic dough.

Leave covered with a damp teacloth for half an hour, then knead again and roll into thin sheets with the rolling-pin. Sprinkle the dough with the cornmeal and let it rest for a few minutes, then roll it out and cut into strips of the desired width.

Tagliatelle are 2 cm wide, fettucine 1 cm, tagliolini a few millimetres, and pappardelle 3 or 4 cm.

Sauces

and dressing

GARLIC BUTTER

◆

150 g butter, 50 g garlic cloves, a few basil leaves.

Chop the garlic and the basil very finely. In a bowl, mix the seasonings with the softened butter and beat to a cream. Wrap it in aluminium foil and put it in the fridge to harden.
If the pieces of garlic are too visible, push the creamy mixture through a fine-mesh sieve before setting it to harden.
Another tip for making sure the garlic is not obtrusively visible in the butter is to blanch the cloves of garlic for a few seconds in boiling water before chopping so that they remain white. Ideal for seasoning pasta and rice dishes.

TRUFFLE BUTTER

◆

150 g butter, 100 g white truffles, salt.

In a bowl, beat the butter until creamy, then add the truffles, which have been cleaned and crushed in a mortar.
Blend the two ingredients well with a pestle or wooden spoon, and season with a pinch of salt.
Wrap the butter in aluminium foil and store in the fridge. Excellent with plain boiled pasta.

BASIL OIL

◆

1 l extra-virgin olive oil, 1 handful basil florets, 10 basil leaves.

Gather the basil florets in the morning, leaving them to dry in the sunlight if they are veiled in dew, and place them in a hermetically-sealed container.
Pour in the oil, close and leave to macerate for 3 weeks in a dark, cool place. Then add the basil leaves and leave the container in its place for another week. Lastly, strain and decant into small bottles. This is an excellent dressing for use with both hot pasta dishes and pasta salads.

GARLIC OIL

◆

1 l oil, 6 large cloves fresh garlic or 4 cloves mature garlic.

Peel the garlic cloves, press them lightly with the back of a knife, place them in a hermetically-sealed container and pour the oil over them.
Close and store in a cool, dark place for about 20 days. Strain, and use to dress pasta salads.

HOT RED PEPPER OIL

◆

1 l extra-virgin olive oil, 3 or 4 hot red peppers, 1 bay leaf.

Crumble the hot red peppers and the bay leaf, and place them in a hermeti-

cally-sealed container, covering them with oil. Leave to steep for about a month in a cool, dark place, then strain. For a spicier flavour, simply leave the oil to steep for longer, while if you prefer a lighter taste you can dilute the flavoured oil with a little fresh oil. Specially recommended for dressing pasta salads.

BÉCHAMEL

◆

50 g butter, 50 g flour, 1/2 l milk, 1 pinch grated nutmeg, salt and pepper.

The correct preparation of a béchamel sauce is one of the first hurdles to be faced by any cook.

The fear of ending up with a lumpy, tasteless liquid will be gradually overcome with experience, and by learning from mistakes.

All it takes is practice, and after a number of attempts you will soon find that you too can make a smooth, tasty béchamel, without even needing to measure the ingredients.

In a saucepan, melt the butter gently over low heat. Sprinkle the flour over it and beat it in using an egg-whisk.

Heat the milk without letting it boil and use it to dilute the sauce. The milk should be added gradually, stirring constantly, to avoid the formation of the dreaded lumps.

Continue stirring rhythmically until you can feel the sauce thickening. As soon as the first boiling bubbles begin to form, count 10 minutes cooking-time, stirring constantly. Just before you switch off the heat, add salt, a grinding of fresh pepper and a pinch of grated nutmeg.

For a thicker sauce, you can increase the quantities of butter and flour (always the same amount of each) while using the same amount of milk, or you can thicken the sauce further by boiling it longer over the heat.

For a very light sauce, the milk can be substituted with vegetable stock, or with fish stock for use with fish-based dishes.

GENOVESE PESTO

◆

1 handful of basil leaves, 1 clove garlic, 1 1/2 tablespoons pine-nuts, 2 teaspoons grated pecorino cheese, 2 teaspoons grated Parmesan cheese, extra-virgin olive oil, salt.

Wash and dry the basil leaves. Place them in a stone mortar with the garlic and pine-nuts (grind the basil leaves by pressing them against the sides of the mortar with the pestle, without actually pounding them).

Continue grinding the ingredients, then add the grated cheeses and a pinch of salt.

As soon as you have a smooth paste, add as much olive oil as required, stirring with the pestle like a spoon to form a thick, creamy sauce. When using the pesto, dilute it with a few spoonfuls of the pasta cooking water. If you prefer, this sauce can also be made successfully in a blender.

Pesto goes perfectly with all kinds of pasta, rice, gnocchi and minestrone. It can be stored in the fridge in hermetically-sealed glass jars, covering the surface with a thin layer of oil, and without the cheeses, which should be added fresh at the moment of use.

PINZIMONIO WITH ROCKET AND PARMESAN CHEESE

◆

3 tablespoons extra-virgin olive oil, 1 1/2 table-spoons lemon juice, 1/2 bunch rocket, 1 clove garlic, Parmesan cheese, salt and pepper.

Carefully blend the oil with the lemon juice and a pinch of salt, then add the finely-chopped rocket and garlic, and season with a twist of freshly-ground pepper. Lastly, add small flakes of Parmesan to the sauce, mixing carefully so as to leave the flakes of cheese intact. Use this sauce to season plain pasta dishes.

MEAT SAUCE WITH BALSAMIC VINEGAR

◆

400 g veal, 100 g bacon, 1 handful dried mush-rooms, 3 peeled tomatoes, 2 celery stalks, 1 onion, 1 carrot, 2 bay leaves, 1 pinch ground cinnamon, 50 g butter, 1 1/2 tablespoon balsamic vinegar, salt, freshly-ground pepper.

Clean and chop the celery stalks, onion and carrot. Place them in a saucepan, add the bacon and butter, and gently sauté the ingredients, stirring constantly with a wooden spoon. Wash the mushrooms and soak them in warm water. Chop the veal into pieces. When the vegetable mixture is gently browned, add the mashed tomatoes and the meat, and let the flavours blend over moderate heat. Lastly, add the well-drained mushrooms, the cinnamon and the bay leaves. Season with salt, freshly-ground pepper and balsamic vinegar. Simmer for about an hour over moderate heat, stirring occasionally.

BASS SAUCE

◆

250 g bass, 200 g ripe and firm tomatoes, 15 g fresh dill, 1 clove garlic, 1 dl cream, dry white wine, extra-virgin olive oil, salt.

In a saucepan, flavour a few tablespoons of oil with the finely-chopped garlic, then add the diced fish and the chopped dill. Let the fish absorb the flavours for a few minutes, then pour in the white wine and let it evaporate. Blanch the tomatoes in boiling water for a few seconds, peel, seed and chop them, and add them to the saucepan. Let the sauce reduce, then dilute with the cream, season with salt, and simmer until the sauce has the right consistency.

GROUPER SAUCE

◆

800 g grouper fillets, 400 g tomato sauce, 1 onion, 1 carrot, 1/2 celery stalk, 1 clove garlic, 1 hot red pepper, 1 bunch parsley, basil, 1/2 glass wine, extra-virgin olive oil, salt.

Clean the fish, removing the skin and bones. Chop the garlic, celery, onion and carrot finely and sauté them in a saucepan in a few spoonfuls of oil, along with the crumbled hot red pepper. Place two slices of fish in the saucepan, pour in the white wine and let it evaporate; break up the fish meat, blending it into the rest of the sauce. Pour in the tomato sauce, season with salt, and simmer for about twenty minutes. Ten minutes before the sauce is done, add the rest of the fish and let it absorb the juices, turning the slices frequently, then remove them with a slotted spoon and set aside. Use the sauce over pasta, drained while still al

dente, sprinkling the dish with chopped parsley and basil. Serve garnished with the pieces of fish.

TOMATO SAUCE

◆

800 g ripe and firm tomatoes, 1 bunch parsley, 1/2 teaspoon sugar, extra-virgin olive oil, salt, hot red pepper.

This is the classic tomato sauce 'pommarola', the sauce par excellence for serving with pasta.
Wash the tomatoes, blanch them in boiling water, remove the skins, stalks and seeds, and pass them through the food-mill. If the tomatoes are very watery, leave them to drain on a sloping surface for at least 15 minutes before puréeing them. Put the tomato purée in a saucepan over moderate heat, adding a dash of oil, and simmer to reduce for about 30 minutes, seasoning with salt and the half-teaspoon of sugar (to counteract the natural acidity). Just before removing from the heat, season with hot red pepper and chopped basil.

Variation

800 g ripe and firm tomatoes, 4 cloves garlic, 1 bunch parsley, oregano (optional), extra-virgin olive oil, hot red pepper, salt.

Peel and purée the tomatoes as in the preceding recipe. In a saucepan, flavour a few spoonfuls of oil with the crushed garlic, being careful not to let the garlic burn and not to over-heat the oil (otherwise, the tomatoes would burn when added).

Lower the heat and add the tomatoes (the garlic can be removed at this stage, if you prefer a milder flavour), then cover the pan and simmer.

After about 20 minutes, season with salt, hot red pepper, chopped parsley and, if you wish, a pinch of oregano.

ASPARAGUS
SAUCE

◆

2 bunches asparagus, 2 teaspoons lemon juice, 2.5 dl milk, grated nutmeg, extra-virgin olive oil, salt and pepper.

Trim the asparagus. Cut the tips and the tender parts of the stems into small pieces, then sauté them in about a ta-blespoon of oil. Season with salt, pep-per and grated nutmeg and add barely half a glass of hot water.

Cover and simmer over moderate heat for about 15 minutes.

As soon as the water has dried out, add the lemon juice. Cook the asparagus un-til they are quite soft, adding the milk gradually. Blend in the blender, then heat up again.

ARTICHOKE
SAUCE

◆

7 artichokes, 50 g salted capers, 50 g black olives, 2 cloves garlic, the juice of 1 lemon, 1 bunch pars-ley, oregano, 2 tablespoons breadcrumbs, 2 teaspoons tamari sauce, extra-virgin olive oil, salt and pepper.

Cut off the stalks and tips of the arti-chokes and remove the tougher outer leaves.

Cut into wedges and soak for a few minutes in water mixed with a little lemon juice.

Drain and blanch for 10 minutes in salt-ed water with lemon juice, then drain again and chop.

Chop the garlic and parsley finely and mix with the breadcrumbs, then sauté for a few minutes in a saucepan with about a tablespoon of oil.

Add the artichokes, stir, then add the pitted olives, the capers rinsed of salt and dried, the tamari sauce, 1 glass of water and a twist of freshly-ground pepper. Lower the heat and simmer covered for about 30 minutes, stirring occasionally.

When the sauce is done, taste it for salt (additional salt may be unnecessary be-cause of the tamari sauce), and season with a little oregano.

ZUCCHINI FLOWER
SAUCE

◆

12 zucchini flowers, 1/2 onion, 1 bunch parsley, 1 pinch saffron powder, 1 egg yolk, grated pecorino cheese, extra-virgin olive oil, salt and pepper.

about twenty minutes. Just before taking it off the heat, add the chopped parsley, the finely sliced garlic, a twist of freshly ground pepper and a dash of olive oil.

SEA-URCHIN SAUCE
◆

30 sea-urchins, 400 g ripe and firm tomatoes, 1 onion, 2 cloves garlic, 1 bunch parsley, a pinch of saffron, extra-virgin olive oil, salt and pepper.

Clean the sea urchins, removing the inner part with the aid of a teaspoon. Chop the onion finely, sauté in plenty of oil, then add the tomatoes (blanched in boiling water, peeled, seeded and coarsely chopped).

Dilute the saffron in a ladleful of hot water or stock and add it to the pan, then season with salt and pepper. Simmer over low heat for 15 minutes, then add the sea-urchin meat and a very finely chopped mixture of parsley and garlic. Remove from the heat when the tomatoes are done, adding a little hot water or stock if the sauce seems too dry.

Heat a few tablespoons of oil in a saucepan, add the finely chopped zucchini flowers, parsley and onion. Add the saffron dissolved in a ladleful of hot water, and a pinch of salt and pepper.

Cook over moderate heat for about 15 minutes, stirring constantly, then blend in a blender or put through the food-mill. Pour the resulting purée back into the saucepan, dilute with a little oil, and heat well. Turn off the heat, cool slightly, then blend in the egg yolk and a few tablespoons of grated pecorino cheese.

PEPPER SAUCE
◆

4 green and yellow peppers, 1 onion, 1 clove garlic, 1 bunch parsley, dry white wine, extra-virgin olive oil, salt and pepper.

Wash the peppers, remove the stalks, seeds and inner membranes, and dice. In a saucepan, soften the chopped onion in a little oil, add the peppers and sauté, stirring constantly with a wooden spoon.

Pour in a little wine, let it evaporate, season with salt and lower the heat. Cover the pan and stew slowly for

THREE CHEESES SAUCE
◆

100 g Gorgonzola, 100 g Fontina, 100 g Gruyère, 1/2 glass cream, béchamel (see page 141), butter, a sprinkle of grated nutmeg, salt and pepper.

Prepare a fairly liquid béchamel sauce. As soon as it is done, stir in the diced cheeses, the cream, a tablespoon of butter, a pinch of salt, a twist of freshly ground pepper, and a sprinkle of grated nutmeg. Continue to heat until you have a fluid, creamy sauce, then switch off. For the classic '4 cheeses' sauce, add a little grated Parmesan.

FISHERMAN'S SAUCE

◆

200 g clams, 200 g mussels, 200 g shrimps, 8 scallops, 3 ripe and firm tomatoes, 1 clove garlic, chives, 1 bunch parsley, 1 1/2 tablespoons extra-virgin olive oil, hot red pepper, salt.

Clean the different types of fish carefully. Soak the mussels and clams in salty water for at least half an hour, then place them in a frying-pan to open over high heat. Remove the shellfish from their shells and strain the cooking juices that have accumulated in the bottom of the pan. Open the scallops and remove the flesh, eliminating the inedible parts and setting the white flesh and the coral roe aside; shell the shrimps. Flavour a few spoonfuls of oil with the crushed garlic clove; as soon as the garlic turns golden, remove it. Add the peeled, seeded and coarsely chopped tomatoes, a crumbled hot red pepper without its seeds, and simmer for a few minutes. Lastly, add the scallops, mussels, clams and shrimps, pouring the cooking juices over the sieved shellfish. Season with salt and simmer for another 5-6 minutes. Before removing from the heat, sprinkle with chopped chives and parsley. If you are using the sauce over pasta, stir it into the saucepan and blend carefully, coating the pasta thoroughly with sauce.

TROUT (OR TENCH) SAUCE

◆

400 g trout (or tench), 200 g tomato sauce, 1 small onion, 1 clove garlic, 1 sprig marjoram, 1 bunch parsley, extra-virgin olive oil, salt, hot red pepper.

Clean the trout and cook it for 10 minutes in boiling salted water, bone it and chop into small pieces. Chop the onion, garlic and marjoram finely, and sauté in a saucepan with about a tablespoon of oil and a little crumbled hot red pepper. Add the tomato sauce, season with salt, and reduce over moderate heat. When the sauce has reduced, add the chopped trout; gently simmer for about 15 minutes. Before removing from the heat, sprinkle with chopped parsley.

SEAFOOD SAUCE

◆

200 g clams, 200 g mussels, 100 g monkfish, 100 g baby squid, 100 g cuttlefish, 3 prawns, 2 shrimps, 1/2 onion, 3 cloves garlic, basil, ginger, 2 glasses dry white wine, extra-virgin olive oil, salt and pepper.

Chop the onion and garlic finely; sauté in a saucepan with plenty of oil. Clean the squid and cuttlefish, cut into pieces and add to the saucepan with the monkfish. Open the clams and mussels in a frying pan over high heat, shell them and add them to the sauce. Lastly, add the prawns and shrimps. Sauté lightly but do not overcook. Pour in the wine and let evaporate over high heat. Season with salt, lower the heat and simmer until done. Add chopped basil and grated ginger just before you switch off the heat.

TOMATO AND OLIVE SAUCE

◆

500 g ripe and firm tomatoes, 150 g black and green olives, 1 1/2 tablespoons of salted capers, 1 clove garlic, oregano or basil, extra-virgin olive oil, salt.

Blanch the tomatoes in boiling water for a few minutes, then peel, seed and chop them. Rinse the salt off the capers under running water and dry them. Chop the garlic finely and sauté in a saucepan with a few spoonfuls of oil, adding the tomatoes before the garlic browns. Then add the green olives, pitted and chopped, the black olives, pitted but whole, and the capers.
Season with salt and simmer over moderate heat. Just before removing from the heat, add the oregano (or chopped basil) and a dash of oil.

EEL AND PEA SAUCE

◆

200 g cleaned eel, 200 g fresh hulled peas, 1 onion, 1 cup tomato sauce, 1 clove garlic, 1 bay leaf, extra-virgin olive oil, salt.

Cut the eel into pieces, chop the onion and sauté them together in a saucepan in a few spoonfuls of oil. When they are evenly coloured, add the tomato sauce and the bay leaf and cook for a few minutes. Stir in the hulled peas and the garlic. Cook the sauce until done, and serve with pasta or polenta.

CHESTNUT AND SAUSAGE SAUCE

◆

20 g ground chestnuts, 200 g sausage, 4 egg yolks, 1/4 l cream, extra-virgin olive oil, salt and pepper.

Peel the sausage, break up the meat with a fork and sauté gently in a saucepan in a few spoonfuls of oil, making sure that it remains soft. Dissolve the ground chestnuts in the cream, and pour into the pan with the sausage meat. In a warmed soup tureen, beat the egg yolks with a pinch of salt and pepper. When the pasta has been cooked and drained, add it to the bowl and mix well. Pour the heated sausage and cream sauce over the pasta, mix well and serve sprinkled with grated Parmesan.

BEAN SAUCE

◆

250 g boiled Borlotti beans, 50 g fatty bacon, 300 g tomato pulp, 1/2 onion, 1 carrot, 1/2 celery stalk, 1 clove garlic, 1 bunch parsley, a few basil leaves, extra-virgin olive oil, salt and pepper.

Chop the bacon along with the parsley and garlic; sauté the mixture in a saucepan with a few spoonfuls of oil. Chop the carrot, celery and onion finely and add to the pan. Cook about 10 minutes, then add the beans. Stir gently, letting the flavours blend. Add the tomato pulp, season with salt and pepper, cover, lower the heat and simmer. Just before removing from the heat, season with a few coarsely chopped basil leaves and a little chopped parsley.

ARTICHOKE, MUSHROOM AND RICOTTA SAUCE

◆

250 g fresh ricotta cheese, 4 artichokes, 200 g fresh mushrooms, 1 shallot, 1 clove garlic, 1 bunch parsley, juice of 1 lemon, 2 teaspoons tomato concentrate (optional), grated Parmesan cheese, dry white wine, extra-virgin olive oil, salt and pepper.

Clean the artichokes, cut off the tips and most of the stalks and remove the tougher outer leaves. Cut into thin wedges and soak in water mixed with a little lemon juice. Clean the mushrooms, removing the earthy residue with a damp cloth, and cut into thin slices. Chop the garlic and shallot finely, sauté in a saucepan with a few spoonfuls of oil, then add the artichokes and mushrooms. Let the flavours blend, stirring constantly over high heat.

After a few minutes, lower the heat, pour in a little white wine and let it evaporate. Season with salt and pepper, cover the saucepan and simmer for about 20 minutes. Add a little hot water if necessary and, if you prefer, the tomato concentrate dissolved in a little hot water. When the sauce is done, add the crumbled ricotta, a few spoonfuls of grated Parmesan and a sprinkle of finely chopped parsley. Mix thoroughly and let the cheeses melt slightly before removing from the heat.

CAULIFLOWER OR BROCCOLI SAUCE

1 cauliflower or a similar amount of broccoli, 1 onion, 2 teaspoons raisins, 2 teaspoons pine-nuts, 2 salted anchovies (optional), grated pecorino cheese, extra-virgin olive oil, hot red pepper, salt.

Either cauliflower or broccoli can be used for this sauce. The classic dish from Puglia is made with broccoli and ore-chiette. Soak the raisins in a little warm water. Separate the florets and blanch them in boiling salted water. Chop the onion and sauté in a saucepan with a few spoonfuls of oil, add the anchovies with the salt rinsed off (optional), and stir until they disintegrate. Add the cauliflower or broccoli florets and simmer until tender, adding hot water if necessary. Before removing from the heat, salt to taste, season with hot red pepper, add the pine-nuts, and the drained and dried raisins. Pour the pasta into the sauce and mix gently. Sprinkle with grated pecorino cheese, or if using fresh pecorino, dice it instead.

SOLE SAUCE

◆

300 g sole fillets, 1 handful basil leaves, 1 dl cream, 1 small shot cognac, vegetable stock, white flour as required, butter, salt and pepper.

Coat the sole fillets lightly with flour and brown them gently in butter in a frying-pan. As soon as they are nicely coloured, pour in the cognac and 2 ladlefuls of hot stock. When the sauce begins to re-

duce, dilute it with the cream, sprinkle with basil, salt and pepper to taste. Pour the drained pasta into the sauce, mixing it in well before serving garnished with a few fresh basil leaves.

HAM AND PEA SAUCE

◆

200 g small hulled peas, 100 g thinly-sliced cooked ham, 1/2 onion, 2 eggs, 2 1/2 tablespoons grated Parmesan cheese, extra-virgin olive oil, salt and pepper.

Chop the onion finely; sauté it in a saucepan in a few spoonfuls of oil, then add the peas, salt and pepper. Lower the heat, cover, and simmer until the peas are tender, adding a little hot water if necessary. Cut the ham into small strips and add to the peas just before removing from the heat, allowing the flavours to blend. In a soup-tureen, beat the eggs with the Parmesan, a pinch of salt and a twist of freshly-ground pepper. When the pasta is done, drain and pour into the tureen, then add and mix well the pea and ham sauce, stirring it in gently.

EGG AND MOZZARELLA SAUCE

◆

4 eggs, 1/2 onion, 1 mozzarella, 50 g grated Parmesan cheese, 1 cup tomato purée, hot red pepper, extra-virgin olive oil, salt.

In a small saucepan, sauté the thinly-sliced onion lightly in a little oil. Add the tomato purée and a pinch of salt, and let reduce for 20 minutes. In the meantime, cook the eggs in a small oiled roasting-tin in a moderate oven. When the pasta is done, drain while still al dente and dress it with the tomato sauce and grated Parmesan. Transfer it to an oiled ovenproof dish, cover with the diced mozzarella and the eggs, sprinkle with a little hot red pepper, and pop into the oven or under the grill for a few minutes until the mozzarella has melted. Remove from the oven and serve.

LAMB SAUCE

📷

200 g lamb, 2 cloves garlic, 1 sprig rosemary, 2 bay leaves, 400 g tomato pulp, red wine, grated pecorino cheese, extra-virgin olive oil, salt and pepper.

Cut the lamb into small pieces and sauté in a saucepan with plenty of oil along with the garlic cloves (which should be removed as soon as they begin to colour), the rosemary and bay leaves. Pour in a little wine and let it evaporate. Then add the tomato pulp, season with salt and pepper and simmer until done over low heat. When the pasta is done, drain and pour it into the sauce, mixing well. Complete the dish with a sprinkle of grated pecorino cheese.

MUSHROOM AND LEEK SAUCE

◆

500 g fresh mushrooms, 2 leeks, 1 bay leaf, 1 clove, 1 bunch parsley, extra-virgin olive oil, salt and pepper.

Clean the vegetables, removing the earthy residue from the mushrooms with a damp cloth. Slice both mushrooms and leeks and put them into a saucepan with a few spoonfuls of oil, the bay leaf, the clove and a pinch of salt. Cover the pan and simmer over low heat, adding a little salted hot water or stock from time to time if necessary. Just before removing from the heat, season with freshly-ground pepper and sprinkle with finely-chopped parsley.

PEAS AND CRESCENZA CHEESE SAUCE

◆

250 g freshly hulled peas, 2 small onions, 1 bunch parsley, 150 g Crescenza cheese, 30 g grated Parmesan cheese, 1 1/2 tablespoons cream, extra-virgin olive oil, salt and pepper.

Clean and chop the onions. Sauté them gently in a saucepan with a few spoonfuls of oil. Add the peas, season with salt and pepper, and add half a glass of hot water. Simmer covered over moderate heat for about 20 minutes, stirring occasionally.
In the meantime, mix the Crescenza in a bowl with the cream, the chopped parsley and the grated Parmesan, beating to form a smooth, creamy mixture. As soon as the peas are done, add the cheese cream. Stirring constantly, letting the cheeses melt over very low heat. Serve with any short type of pasta.

OYSTER SAUCE

◆

16 oysters, 12 scallops, 1 shallot, 1/2 glass Champagne, 60 g butter, salt, white pepper.

Open the oysters, clean them and extract the flesh, working over a pan to collect their liquid, which should then be strained. Shell and trim the scallops, discarding the inedible parts and retaining only the white flesh and the coral roe.
In a saucepan, wilt the finely-chopped shallot in butter, and immediately pour in the champagne. Let the flavours mingle for a few minutes, then add the scallops, removing them after a few minutes with a slotted spoon.
Stir the sauce thoroughly, dilute with the oyster water, heat it up again, then add the oysters and reheat the scallops too for a few minutes. Salt to taste and season with a twist of freshly-ground white pepper, letting the flavours blend for a few minutes before using.

TUNA SAUCE ALL'ARRABBIATA

◆

150 g tuna in oil, 2 salted anchovies, 500 g tomato purée, 50 g black olives, 2 teaspoons capers, 2 cloves garlic, 1 handful basil leaves, 1 pinch thyme, extra-virgin olive oil, hot red pepper, salt.

Break up the tuna with a fork and sauté it in a saucepan with a little oil. Add the tomato purée and a little crumbled hot red pepper. Flavour with thyme and let the sauce reduce. Rinse the anchovies free of salt, remove any bones, then chop them with the capers. When the sauce is done, add the anchovies, the pounded basil, the garlic and the olives. Add salt and let the flavours blend before removing from the heat.

MULLET SAUCE

◆

300 g mullet fillets, 3 ripe and firm tomatoes, 2 cloves garlic, ginger, 1 bunch parsley, 1/2 glass dry white wine, extra-virgin olive oil, salt.

In a saucepan, flavour a few spoonfuls of oil with the clove of garlic; as soon as the garlic begins to colour, remove it. Add the mullet cut into pieces along with the ginger, and sauté. Blanch the tomatoes in boiling water, then peel, seed and chop them. Add them to the fish when the wine has almost entirely evaporated. Salt to taste, simmer for 15 minutes, and complete with a sprinkle of chopped parsley.

CLAM AND TOMATO SAUCE

◆

500 g clams, 5 anchovies, 600 g ripe and firm tomatoes, 3 cloves of garlic, a few basil leaves, 1/2 glass dry white wine, extra-virgin olive oil, hot red pepper, salt.

Soak the clams in salted water for at least half an hour, then rinse them carefully. Place a large frying pan on the heat, add the clams and pour the wine over them. As soon as the clams open, drain and shell them. Strain the cooking juices well and set aside. Clean and fillet the anchovies; in a saucepan, stir them in hot oil with the crumbled hot red pepper until they disintegrate.

Blanch the tomatoes in boiling water, peel, seed and chop them, then add them to the sauce along with the cooking juices of the clams. Season with salt and let the sauce reduce. When the sauce is done, add the clams along with the finely-chopped garlic and basil.

ZUCCHINI SAUCE

◆

3 zucchini, 1 bunch parsley or a few mint leaves, 1 clove garlic, grated hard ricotta cheese, extra-virgin olive oil, ground hot red pepper, salt.

Wash the zucchini and slice them thinly. In a non-stick saucepan, heat a few spoonfuls of olive oil, add the zucchini slices and brown them evenly.

When they are nearly done, add salt and a pinch of hot red pepper, the sliced garlic and the finely chopped parsley.

153

Drain the pasta (long types are recommended with this sauce) while still al dente and mix it with the zucchini sauce, adding a dash of fresh oil and a sprinkle of grated ricotta.

ZUCCHINI AND PEA SAUCE

4 zucchini, 250 g freshly hulled peas, 2 leeks, 1 bunch parsley, basil, 2 tablespoons cream, extra-virgin olive oil, salt and pepper.

Slice the leeks. Sauté them in a saucepan with a few tablespoons of oil, adding the peas before the leeks begin to brown. Wash, dry and slice the zucchini not too thinly, stirring the slices into the sauce when it has cooked for about 5 minutes.

Let the flavours blend, lower the heat, season with salt and a grinding of fresh pepper, cover the pan and simmer for about 30 minutes. Stir well and, if necessary, add a little hot stock or water from time to time.

When the sauce is done, sprinkle with chopped parsley and a few roughly-torn basil leaves, add the cream, and heat well before switching off.

COLD AVOCADO SAUCE

◆

2 ripe avocados, the juice of 2 lemons, 2 cloves garlic, basil, coriander, 1 glass extra-virgin olive oil, hot red pepper, salt.

Peel the avocados and cut the flesh into pieces, then blend it in the blender with the garlic, the oil, the strained lemon juice, a few leaves of basil, a pinch of coriander, one of salt and one of hot red pepper. The sauce is now ready to be served with the pasta of your choice.

COLD ROCKET SAUCE

◆

1 bunch rocket, 2.5 dl of cream, 75 g grated Parmesan cheese, 75 g fresh soft cheese (ricotta, caprino, etc.), salt and pepper.

In a bowl, blend the cheeses with the cream, seasoning with salt and a grinding of pepper, until you have a smooth cream. Add the coarsely chopped rocket, diluting the mixture if it is too stiff with a few spoonfuls of the pasta cooking water.

Remember that if you use wild rocket, you should use less since it has a much stronger flavour than the cultivated variety. Wild rocket should always be gathered in places free from atmospheric pollution.

154

Recipe index